Professional Stage

Module F

Financial Strategy

Examination Notes

British Library Cataloguing-in-Publication Data

A catalogue record for this book is available from the British Library.

Published by AT Foulks Lynch Ltd
Number 4
The Griffin Centre
Staines Road
Feltham
TW14 0HS

ISBN 0 7483 3483 1

© AT Foulks Lynch Ltd, 1996

PREFACE

These Examination Notes have been written specifically for the Financial Strategy paper of the ACCA examinations.

They follow the ACCA Official **Teaching Guide** closely. All the major elements of the Guide are covered in detail to provide excellent revision for students in their final preparation for the examinations.

CONTENTS

Session 1   *Financial Strategy: Its Nature and Scope*

1.1   **Describe what is meant by financial strategy**

Remember the usual distinction between strategy, tactics and operational control.

Strategy is 'a course of action, including the specification of resources required, to achieve a specific objective'.

Tactics are 'the most efficient deployment of resources in an agreed strategy'.

Operational control is 'the management of daily activities in accordance with strategic and tactical plans'.

Senior management select the strategy
Middle managers decide the tactics
Line managers carry out the operational control.

1.2   **Identify the importance of financial strategy to the organisation**

Financial strategy is that area of a company's strategy within the scope of the financial managers, including:

❑   from which sources should funds be raised?

❑   should proposed investments be undertaken?

❑   how large a dividend should be paid?

❑   how should working capital be controlled eg, should discounts be offered to debtors for prompt payment?

❑   should hedging strategies be adopted to avoid currency or interest rate risk?

1.3   **Discuss the relationship between financial strategy and overall corporate strategy**

A company's overall corporate strategy will be a portfolio of different strategies designed to carry out a long-term plan of action to attain specified objectives. It is therefore of critical importance to consider the possible objectives of organisations.

1.4   **Identify the aims and objectives of organisations**

❑   In most exam questions the maximisation of shareholders' wealth will be assumed

❑   But may need to discuss alternative concepts

Maximising and satisficing:

- ❑   Maximising means seeking best possible outcome

- ❑   Satisficing = adequate outcome

- ❑   Maximisation normally assumed

1.5   Describe the goals of different interest groups

Whose returns are we maximising?

- ❑   Community

- ❑   Employees

- ❑   Management

- ❑   Ordinary shareholders

Last option assumed, but often relaxed in decision making process.

Each of the interest groups is likely to have different objectives:

- ❑   Community may want low pollution and high involvement in local issues eg, supporting local charities.

- ❑   Employees want high wages and continuity of their employment.

- ❑   Management want high wages and may want the company to be as large as possible so that they can 'empire-build'.

- ❑   Ordinary shareholders want high dividends and growth in the share price.

    Other interest groups which might be considered are trade suppliers, trade customers, debt providers, government, etc.

1.6 **Understand the significance of changing share ownership patterns for the company**

Consider the following table:

Percentage holdings of UK listed equities held by different groups

	1963 %	1973 %	1983 %	1989 %
Insurance companies	11	16	22	25
Pension funds	7	12	29	29
Investment trusts	9	10	6	3
Unit trusts	1	3	4	6
Total institutions	28	41	61	63
Persons	59	42	25	18
Others	13	17	14	19
	100	100	100	100

The lesson is that, despite the government's privatisation programme, individual direct shareholdings have fallen while institutional shareholdings have increased.

The reasons for this trend can be summarised as

❑ tax advantages of institutional investment

❑ growth in occupational pension schemes

❑ growth in unit trusts

❑ individuals have concentrated their savings in their houses

❑ stockbrokers have marketed to institutions rather than cultivating private investors.

1.7 **Define the meaning of corporate governance from a UK perspective and briefly contrast between UK practices and those of other countries especially the USA, Continental Europe and the Far East**

The Committee on the Financial Aspects of Corporate Governance (the Cadbury committee) defines corporate governance as 'the system by which companies are directed and controlled'.

Developments in corporate governance in the UK have been slow in recent years, though the establishment of the Cadbury committee in May 1991 and the publication of the Cadbury report in December 1992 has bounced the topic into the forefront of UK debate.

❑ USA practice:

  ❑ SEC imposes quarterly reporting requirements

  ❑ all listed companies are required to have an audit committee.

❑ German practice:

  ❑ large companies generally have a two-tier board system, with separate management board and supervisory board

  ❑ banks providing credit to a company will often hold a long-term equity stake in the company.

❑ Japanese practice:

  ❑ traditionally companies wishing to do business with each other will buy shares in each other to symbolise their long-term relationship. Many companies were therefore sheltered from the attentions of external shareholders requiring dividends and interested in day-to-day matters. However the system of cross-holdings is now reducing.

1.8 Understand the debate regarding corporate governance, including the Cadbury report

The Financial Reporting Council (FRC), London Stock Exchange and the accountancy profession set up a committee under the chairmanship of Sir Adrian Cadbury in May 1991 to propose improvements to UK corporate governance.

The Cadbury report was published in December 1992. The boards of all UK listed companies are now required to comply with the Code of Best Practice contained in the report.

The code contains the following provisions:

❑ The board of directors should meet regularly, retain full and effective control over the company and monitor the executive management. The board should include non-executive directors.

❑ The non-executive directors should bring an independent judgement to bear on issues of strategy, performance, resources, including key appointments, and standards of conduct. Their fees should reflect the time which they commit to the company, they should be appointed for specified terms and reappointment should not be automatic.

❑ Executive directors' service contracts should not exceed three years without shareholders' approval. Executive directors' pay should be subject to the recommendations of a remuneration committee made up wholly or mainly of non-executive directors.

❑ An audit committee should be established of at least three non-executive directors to liaise with the external auditors.

1.9 Identify the role of auditors, audit committees, non-executive directors etc, in corporate governance

❑ external auditors are required by the Companies Act to give their opinion on whether the company's financial statements give a true and fair view.

❑ internal auditors carry out specific tasks for management as part of the company's internal controls.

❑ the audit committee should carry out the following duties

    ❑ recommend to the board the appointment of auditors, and the level of audit fee

    ❑ liaise with the external auditors

    ❑ review the work of internal auditors and receive their reports

    ❑ review the management letter received from the external auditors

    ❑ review the company's statement on the system of internal controls.

Session 2   *Conflicts of Interest and their Resolution*

2.1   Identify directors' powers and behaviour, including the significance of creative accounting, off-balance sheet finance and the influence of the threat of take-over

Shareholders entrust the day-to-day management of their company to directors. The directors will generally set their own agenda to run the business; shareholders are entitled to attend AGMs and challenge the directors but in practice this seldom occurs.

Directors may be remunerated by a bonus system based on the company's profitability. They will therefore be motivated to report high short-term profits, perhaps at the expense of long-term profitability. Similar arguments apply if their company is vulnerable to take-over. Reporting high short-term profits should drive up the value of the business and discourage predators.

However in the 1980s several managements took this process too far and flattered their reported profits by indulging in creative accounting eg, the use of leased assets rather than purchased assets, or the use of quasi-subsidiaries. The developing work of the ASB should discourage these practices in the 1990s eg, the virtual abolition of extraordinary items in FRS 3 and the requirement to consolidate quasi-subsidiaries in FRS 5.

2.2   Understand the principles of agency theory and their contribution to the debate on governance

The shareholders have appointed the directors as their agents to run the company. There is an agency relationship in law between the two parties. Agency theory examines this relationship and postulates that the company can be viewed as a set of contracts between each of the various interest groups. Although each member of each group might act in his own self-interest, the groups as a whole (ie, the company) will not thrive unless all the groups comprising the company are performing well.

For example, managers must see it to be in their interests for the company to prosper in the long-term, so they should not just seek to boost short-term profits.

2.3   Understand the potential for conflict between owners, directors, managers and other interest groups

This has already been examined above in Session 1.

2.4   Discuss the meaning of goal congruence, and understand how it might be achieved through the use of alternative reward systems including share option schemes and profit related pay

Goal congruence exists where each of the units within a business (ie, individual employees, managers, directors, departments etc) is seeking to achieve personal objectives which are also in the best interests of the business as a whole. To persuade managers that a company's long-term strength should be pursued, remuneration schemes may be based on growth in a company's share price. For options granted under an approved scheme, there is no tax charge when the option is granted (at the current market value) and also no tax charge when the option is exercised, providing that options are exercised between three and ten years after they are granted, and not more frequently than once in three years.

2.5   Discuss the role of non-executive directors, administrators etc, with respect to the organisation

The role of non-executive directors has been covered in the Cadbury report. The organisation PRO NED exists to promote the role of non-executive directors in UK business. Historically non-executive directors have often been chosen by the chairman from amongst his golfing friends; this is no longer acceptable.

Session 3   *Translating Market Disciplines*

3.1   Explain and quantify what is meant by adequate financial return, contrasting profit based measures with net present value of expected cash flows

❑   in practice shareholders will have a satisficing objective ie, they will seek a satisfactory return from an investment

❑   similarly companies will seek a satisfactory return from projects that they undertake.

There are several ways in which an adequate financial return could be measured

❑   Profits
❑   Profits per share
❑   ROCE
❑   Dividends
❑   Dividend + capital growth

Last item is accepted measure of shareholders' wealth.

Since profits can be distorted by the selection of different accounting policies and by inflation, measures of return based on cash flows are preferred.

3.2   Understand the benefits of using net present value, and how the use of net present value can serve as a unifying long term objective for the enterprise as a whole

The assumed primary corporate objective is generally the maximisation of shareholder wealth. Fundamental analysis implies that shareholder wealth equals the net present value of cash flows arising. NPV analysis can therefore unite shareholders and management in a common objective.

Other measures of project return are possible:

	Advantages	*Disadvantages*
(i) Payback		
$\dfrac{\text{Project investment}}{\text{Annual cash flow}}$	Easy to understand	Ignores time value of money
The number of years it takes to recoup the initial investment	Uses earlier cash flows which are more certain	Ignores cash flows after payback period
	Uses cash flows not profits	Difficulty in finding a target period

Useful measure if short of cash

(ii)   Accounting rate of return

$$\frac{\text{Average annual profit} \times 100}{\text{Project investment}}$$

% return on investment in terms of accounting profit	Easy to understand	Ignores time value of money
	Percentage result more acceptable to management	Does not use cash flows
	Business is judged by ROI by financial markets	Ambiguity over definitions in formula
	Management often judged on ROI	Difficulty in finding a target ARR

(iii)   Net present value

Calculate using formula or tables	Uses time value of money	Not easily understood by management
Accept only projects with positive NPV or rank mutually exclusive projects in order of NPV	Unambiguous criteria for accept/reject decision	Requires cost of capital
	Direct link with assumed objective of investment appraisal	

3.3   Revise NPV analysis, including the identification of relevant cash flows and the impact of price level changes

❑   NPV is based on cash flows, not profits

❑   exclude non-cash flow credits and charges eg, depreciation

❑   ignore sunk costs

❑   relevant costs are opportunity costs and incremental cash flows

❑   deal with inflation by either discounting money flows at the money rate, or real flows at the real rate. Do not mix them up.

3.4   Describe the efficient markets hypothesis including weak, semi-strong and strong form efficiency

❑   Weak form

Share prices reflect all the information contained in the record of past prices. As a result it is not possible to predict future share price movements by reference to past trends. Share prices follow a random walk

❑   Semi-strong form

Share prices also reflect all current publicly available information. Therefore prices will change only when new information is published. As a result it would only be possible to predict share price movements if unpublished information were known (insider dealing)

❑   Strong form

Share prices reflect all information that is relevant to the company

If this is the case then share price movements can never be predicted

Gains through insider dealing are not possible because shares are priced absolutely fairly

3.5   Understand the meaning of market efficiency and its significance to financial decision-making based upon NPV

❑   Definition

❑   An efficient market is one in which the market price of all securities traded on it reflects all the available information

❑   If this is correct, a company's real financial position, with respect to both current and future profitability, will be reflected in its share price

❑   Implications of EMH

❑   Markets have no memory

The pattern of past price changes contains no information about future changes

❑   Trust market prices

In an efficient market they reflect all available information and are fairly valued

> ❑   There are no financial illusions
>
> Investors are concerned only with the company's cash flows ie, changes in accounting or dividend policies are irrelevant
>
> ❑   The 'do-it-yourself' alternative
>
> Mergers are often justified on the basis that they result in a more diversified and more stable firm, but investors can achieve their own diversification by holding different securities
>
> ❑   Seen one share, seen them all
>
> Investors buy a share because it offers a fair return for its risk, not for any specific qualities. Therefore shares should be close to perfect substitutes for each other such that if the return on one is too low relative to its risk, nobody will want to hold that share, and vice versa if the return is too high
>
> ❑   Reading the entrails
>
> Since market prices reflect all available information, a study of their detailed build up may be used to make predictions about the future.

3.6 Explain the meaning of the term structure of interest rates, including the forms of the yield curve and the expectations, liquidity preference and market segmentation theories

Definition

The term structure of interest rates refers to the way in which the yield of a security varies according to the term of the security ie, to the length of time before the borrowing will be repaid.

Normally, the longer the term of a security, the higher will be its gross redemption yield (ie, interest yield plus capital gain or loss to maturity).

Check that this is the case by looking at the 'UK Gilts Prices' section of the Financial Times. The redemption yield on shorts will normally be less than the redemption yield of mediums and longs.

The 'yield curve' at any time shows the graph of gilts' redemption yields plotted against the term of each gilt.

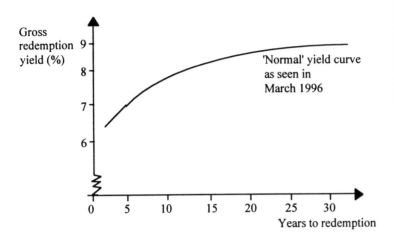

For example a gilt with five years before redemption could be expected to yield just over 7% pa until redemption, while a 20 year gilt would yield nearly 8½%.

The 'normal' form of yield curve is upwards sloping as shown in the graph. This can be explained by investors' liquidity preference ie, the fact that investors need to be compensated with a higher yield for being deprived of their cash for a longer period of time.

Unusually the yield curve might become 'inverted' ie, downwards sloping. This arises when the expectations of investors generally are that interest rates are going to fall, so that short-term rates are higher than long-term rates.

A further factor affecting the shape of the yield curve is market segmentation theory. This suggests that different categories of investors are interested in different segments of the curve (eg, building societies in the short end and pension funds in the long end). The two ends of the curve might therefore react differently to the same set of economic news.

3.7   Understand the significance of yield curves to financial managers

Financial managers should inspect yield curves primarily to assess the market's expectations of future movements in interest rates.

Session 4   *The Valuation of Securities*

4.1   Understand models for the valuation of shares and bonds, dividend growth models, earnings growth models and use such models to estimate value from given information

All formulae use the fundamental relationship that the value of a security equals the present value of the expected cash inflows arising from owning the security.

Formulae

❑   Constant dividends

$$E_0 = \frac{d}{k}$$

❑   Constant dividend growth

$$E_0 = \frac{d_0(1+g)}{k-g}$$

Estimating g

❑   Extrapolation of past dividends ie, dividend growth model eg,

$$g = \sqrt[4]{d_0 \div \text{Dividend 4 years ago}} - 1$$

❑   Earnings growth model

$$g \quad = \quad br; \ b = \frac{EAIT - d_0}{EAIT}$$

$$r \quad =$$

$$\frac{EAIT}{\text{Opening value of equity @ historical cost}}$$

Symbols

k	=	the shareholders' cost of capital
E_0	=	ex dividend market value of equity
d	=	total annual dividend payment
d_0	=	total current dividend
g	=	dividend growth rate
b	=	retention rate
r	=	return on reinvested funds

$$\text{EAIT} = \text{earnings after interest and tax}$$
$$= \text{EPS} \times \text{number of shares}$$

Notes:

❏ Remember that E_0 is the ex div market value

Ex div MV = Cum div MV - d_o

❏ For determining g from past dividends, look out for the relevant period eg, dividend growth over a 4 year period will give 5 dividend figures

❏ PE ratio $= \dfrac{E_0}{\text{EAIT}}$

Dividend cover $= \dfrac{\text{EAIT}}{d}$

❏ Similar formulae apply for irredeemable bonds as they do for shares

Example

Podge plc has just paid a dividend of 14p per share. Two years previously the dividend was 12p per share. The company's shareholders have a cost of capital of 16%. Estimate the fair value of the share price.

Answer

$$12 (1 + g)^2 = 14$$
$$g = 8\%$$

$$E_0 = \frac{14(1.08)}{0.16 - 0.08}$$

$$= 189\text{p}$$

Example

Podge plc also has irredeemable 10% debentures. Tax is payable at 33% and investors continue to require 16% on their investments. Estimate the fair value of a £100 debenture.

$$\text{Fair value} = \frac{\text{Net interest}}{\text{Cost of capital}}$$

$$= \frac{£10 \times (1 - 0.33)}{0.16}$$

$$= £41.88$$

4.2   Be aware of the theoretical and practical limitations of such models

❑   assumption of constant future growth rate could be wrong

❑   investors are assumed to be rational and risk-averse

❑   ignores asset values

❑   ignores earnings values

❑   ignores investors' different tax positions

4.3   Discuss the relevance of accounting information to share valuation

❑   shares can be valued using PE values

Price per share = EPS × agreed PE ratio

❑   however accounting information is based on the past, whereas in buying a share one is buying a series of future cash flows

4.4   Be aware of practical influences on share prices, including reasons why share prices differ from their theoretical values

❑   good asset backing ie, high net asset value per share

❑   level of earnings

❑   technical factors eg, a larger number of sellers than buyers one day will tend to drive the price down

❑   changes in forecasts taking time to disseminate through the market

❑   distrust of particular management figures eg, some fund managers always refused to own shares in companies run by Robert Maxwell.

4.5   Understand and apply models for the valuation of debt and other securities

The principles of valuing debt as the present value of the cash flows arising are exactly the same as for shares.

Irredeemable debt

$$E_0 = \frac{I}{k}$$

Where

E_0	=	ex int market value of debt
I	=	interest payments
k	=	the required return

Redeemable debt

E_0 = present value of interest payments + present value of redemption amount

Convertible loan stock

Value at the higher of entry value into equity and value as a straight loan stock.

Warrants

Value at the excess of entry value into equity over the current equity price.

Session 5   *Portfolio Theory*

5.1   Understand the benefits of portfolio diversification

Diversification reduces risk. Investors are assumed to be risk averse, so diversification pleases investors by offering expected returns at lower risk than individual securities.

The better the negative correlation between the investments, the better the diversification (eg, umbrellas and swimming costumes).

5.2   Estimate the risk and return of portfolios

Two asset portfolios

(a)   Return and risk

Return	= weighted average of individual security returns
Risk is not equal to	weighted average of individual security standard deviations (unless perfectly positively correlated) (anything less than perfect positive correlation results in risk reduction)

(b)   Formulae

(i)   Variance, Var $\qquad = \Sigma p(x - \bar{x})^2$

(ii)   Standard deviation, $\sigma \qquad = \sqrt{\text{var}}$

(iii)   Expected value, x $\qquad = \Sigma px$

(iv)   Covariance, $\text{Cov}_{xy} \qquad = \Sigma p(x - \bar{x})(y - \bar{y})$

$$\text{or} \qquad = \frac{\Sigma xy - n.\bar{x}\,\bar{y}}{n}$$

(v)   Correlation, $\text{Cor}_{xy} \qquad = \dfrac{\text{Covariance}_{x,y}}{\sigma_x \sigma_y}$

$$\text{or} \qquad = \frac{\Sigma xy - n\bar{x}\,\bar{y}}{n(\sigma_x)(\sigma_y)}$$

(vi)   Return on a two asset portfolio,

$$\bar{r} = x_A \bar{r}_A + (1 - x_A)\bar{r}_B$$

(vii)   Risk of a two asset portfolio,

$$\sigma p = \sqrt{x_A{}^2 \sigma_A{}^2 + (1-x_A)^2 \sigma_B{}^2 + 2x_A(1-x_A)Cor_{AB}\sigma_A\sigma_B}$$

5.3   Understand the meaning of mean-variance efficiency for two asset portfolios and portfolios of many assets, efficient portfolios and the efficient frontier

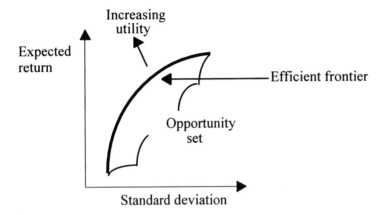

A portfolio is mean-variance efficient if it offers the maximum return for a given level of risk, or the minimum risk for a given level of return.

All efficient portfolios lie on the efficient frontier.

5.4   Understand the concept of utility and its importance to portfolio selection

Investors are each assumed to be trying to maximise their own personal utility. Indifference curves can be drawn for a particular investor showing combinations of risks and returns that offer that investor equal satisfaction ie, equal utility. An investor will therefore choose the portfolio on the efficient frontier which cuts the highest indifference curve on the graph to maximise his utility.

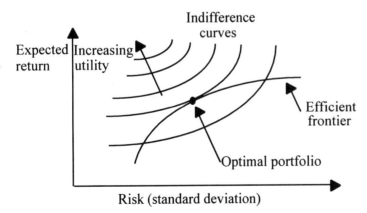

5.5 **Explain portfolio selection when both risky and risk free assets are available**

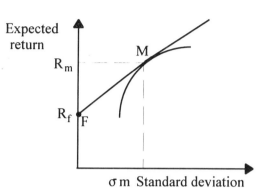

Capital market line =
new efficient frontier =
market price of risk

R_f = risk free rate
= return on treasury bills

R_m = return on market portfolio
= return on FT all share index

σ_m = σ on market portfolio
= σ on FT all share index

Equation of CML:

$$R_j = R_f + \frac{(R_m - R_f)\,\sigma_j}{\sigma_m}$$

Slope = The market price of risk

Investors can now choose a combination of risk free securities (eg, government-backed Treasury Bills) and risky securities (the whole stock market). The straight line FM and beyond becomes the new efficient frontier.

5.6 **Discuss the nature and significance of the Capital Market Line**

This line joining the risk free rate (point F) to a portfolio of all quoted shares (point M) and beyond is called the Capital Market Line. It is the efficient frontier comprising efficient combinations of risk free and risky investments. Individual investors should select the point along this line at which their utility is maximised.

5.7 **Discuss the relevance of portfolio theory to practical financial management**

Problems

❑ need to assess the risk/return preferences of shareholders

❑ portfolio theory is only a single time period model

❑ forecasting returns and the correlations between returns is difficult

However it is valuable for managers to appreciate the benefits of diversification, especially in unquoted companies where the shares might comprise a large proportion of the shareholders' wealth. Larger companies should not be so keen on diversification, since their shareholders can become diversified by buying a selection of shares in different companies rather than relying on the companies themselves being diversified.

5.8   **Discuss the limitations of portfolio theory**

❑   problems mentioned above

❑   measuring risk as the standard deviation of expected returns is not the whole story; there are other costs (eg, the risk of bankruptcy) associated with high risk investment strategies.

Session 6   The Capital Asset Pricing Model

6.1   Understand the meaning and significance of systematic and unsystematic risk

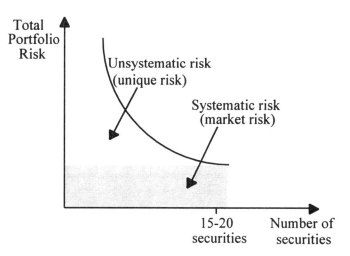

❑   systematic risk depends on the market as a whole

❑   unsystematic risk is unique to each company's shares

Unsystematic risk can be eliminated by holding a diversified portfolio.

6.2   Discuss the Security Market Line

Only systematic risk commands returns in an efficient market.

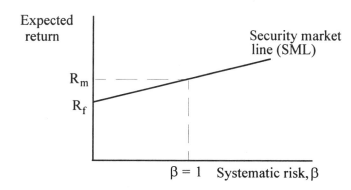

Equation of SML

$$R_j = R_f + \beta (R_m - R_f)$$

6.3 Understand what is meant by alpha and beta factors, their interpretation and how they are calculated

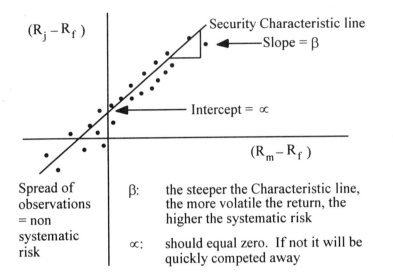

| Spread of observations = non systematic risk | β: | the steeper the Characteristic line, the more volatile the return, the higher the systematic risk |
| | ∝: | should equal zero. If not it will be quickly competed away |

By regression

$$\text{Slope of line} = \beta_j = \frac{\text{cov}_{jm}}{\text{Var}_m}$$

$$= \frac{\text{Correlation Coefficient}_{jm} \; \sigma_j \sigma_m}{\text{Var}_m}$$

$$= \frac{\text{Correlation Coefficient}_{jm} \; \sigma_j}{\sigma_m}$$

❑ ∝ = the abnormal return ie, the return observed greater than that forecast by CAPM. Sometimes also called the rate of price appreciation

❑ β = a measurement of the systematic risk

6.4 Discuss the problems of using historic data as the basis for future decision-making, and evidence of the stability of beta over time

Beta is calculated statistically from past observed returns

❑ the longer the period inspected, the better

❑ the more data inspected, the better, so perhaps use a sector average β rather than just one company's β.

Beta will only be stable if the company's systematic risk remains stable ie, the company carries on the same areas of business - research indicates that betas are more or less constant over time.

6.5   Describe the assumptions of CAPM

❑   total risk can be split between systematic risk and unsystematic risk

❑   unsystematic risk can be completely diversified away

❑   a risk free security exists

❑   beta values remain constant throughout time

6.6   Understand the uses of the model in financial management

❑   CAPM enables a required discount rate to be calculated for capital investment projects on the basis of the projects' systematic risk.

CAPM can be used to 'tailor make' discount rates to the systematic risk of projects which differ from the current business risk of the firm

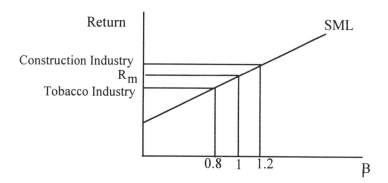

Betas for project appraisal can be obtained by

❑   Using βs of companies operating in similar areas to the proposed project

❑   Forecasting project returns, market returns and calculating a project β from first principles

Warning   When using betas from other firms, care must be exercised to ensure they are as similar as possible to the project. Watch out for differences in size, operating gearing and financial gearing

❑   Note that differences in financial gearing can be adjusted for by using M & M equations.

❏   CAPM enables a company's cost of equity to be estimated from the equation

$$k_e = r_f + \beta_{equity} \, (r_m - r_f)$$

where β_{equity} is the observed beta of the shares in question.

❏   CAPM enables the performance of fund managers to be assessed to see if their actual return exceeded the return expected from the model.

6.7   Discuss the limitations of the model, including some of the instances when it does not perform as expected (eg, low beta investments, low PE investments, day of week effects etc)

❏   views income and capital returns as equally attractive

❏   ignores unsystematic risk, which may be of interest to investors who do not hold a diversified portfolio

❏   is a single period model

❏   what rate to choose for r_f?

❏   what β to choose?

❏   in practice the basic CAPM appears not to work accurately for investments with very high or very low betas, overstating the required return for high beta securities and understating the required return for low beta securities.   However this problem mostly disappears when the effects of taxation are introduced to develop the basic model.

❏   similarly, CAPM does not seem to generate accurate forecasts for returns for companies with low PEs, and ignores seasonal effects. For example, May is usually a bad month for the stock market (sell in May and go away) while January is a good month. Such anomalies cannot be justified by CAPM.

Session 7   The Cost of Capital

7.1   Estimate the cost of equity, using the CAPM and dividend valuation models

The formulae use the same fundamental analysis as in the valuation of securities above.

Cost of equity

❑   Constant dividends

$$k_e = \frac{d}{E_0}$$

❑   Constant dividend growth

$$k_e = \frac{d_0(1+g)}{E_0} + g$$

where
k_e = the cost of equity
E_0 = ex div market value of equity
d = total annual dividend payment
d_0 = total current dividend
g = dividend annual growth rate, estimated either by extrapolating the previous observed growth rate, or by the earnings growth model $g = rb$.

❑   Capital asset pricing model

$$k_e = r_f + \beta_{equity}\,(r_m - r_f)$$

where
r_f = risk free rate
r_m = expected return on market portfolio
β_{equity} = company (equity) β

7.2   Estimate the cost of debt, for both redeemable and irredeemable debt

Formulae

❑   Irredeemable debt

$$k_d = \frac{I(1-T)}{D_0}$$

❏ Redeemable debt

k_d of loan stock redeemable at t_n is the internal rate of return of the following cash flows (assuming tax relief is immediate)

t_0 (Ex Interest Market Price)
$t_{1 \to n}$ Interest $\times (1-T)$
t_n Redemption price

❏ Preference share capital

Fixed dividend (cf irredeemable debt)

$$\text{Cost of preference share capital} = \frac{\text{Annual dividend}}{\text{Ex dividend MV}}$$

❏ Convertible loan stock

If the option to convert into ordinary shares at t_n is exercised, the cost is the IRR of the following cash flows

t_o (Ex interest market value of debt)
$t_{1 \to n}$ Interest $\times (1 - T)$
t_n Market value of ordinary shares into which the debt is to be converted.

❏ Bank loans and overdrafts

Cost = interest rate $\times (1 - T)$

Symbols

k_d =   cost of debt
D_0 =   ex interest market value of debt
I =   total annual interest payment
T =   rate of corporation tax

Notes:

❏ The cash flows for the determination of the cost of redeemable (and irredeemable) debt would need to be adapted if there were a lag in the tax relief

❏ Preference dividends are payable from post-tax profits and therefore should not be reduced by tax in the formula

❏ If no conversion ratio is given for convertible loan stock, it must be assumed that it will remain as debt

7.3 **Understand the weighted average cost of capital of a company, and how it is estimated**

(a)   Formula for WACC

$$k \quad = \quad \frac{Ek_e + Dk_d}{E + D}$$

Note: this may be expanded to incorporate other forms of financing, based on the respective market values

(b)   When should WACC be used?

    (i)   When applicable

        ❑   Company's funds - pool of resources

        ❑   New project financed from pool

    (ii)   When not applicable

        ❑   Projects with different business risk to company

        ❑   Projects with different finance risk ie, financed in a different way from the company

        ❑   Project specific finance eg, government subsidy or grant

(c)   Calculation difficulties

    (i)   Cost of equity

        Dividend valuation model

        ❑   Validity of share price = discounted value of future dividends

        ❑   Current share price must be in equilibrium

        ❑   Validity of constant dividends or constant growth of dividends

        ❑   Determination of g

        Capital asset pricing model

        ❑   see CAPM later

(ii)   Cost of debt and other forms of capital

Debt

  ❑ Validity of market value = discounted future cash flows

  ❑ Current market value must be in equilibrium

Convertible loan stock

  ❑ Will it be converted into shares?

  ❑ Determination of market value of shares at conversion date

Bank loans/overdrafts

  ❑ Variable interest rates

(iii)   General

  ❑ Distinction between short-term and permanent finance eg, overdraft - if only for working capital, do not include in WACC

7.4 Discuss the theories of Modigliani and Miller including their assumptions, and the value and limitations of their theories and their implications for the capital structure decision

(a)   Operating and financial gearing

$$\text{Operating gearing} \quad = \quad \frac{\%\text{ change in EBIT}}{\%\text{ change in sales}}$$

$\Rightarrow$ higher fixed costs, higher operating gearing

Financial gearing

  ❑ Capital: $\dfrac{D}{E}$ or $\dfrac{D}{E+D}$

   - could also be based on book values

  ❑ Income: $\dfrac{EBIT}{\text{Debt interest}}$ (Interest cover)

(b)   The traditional view

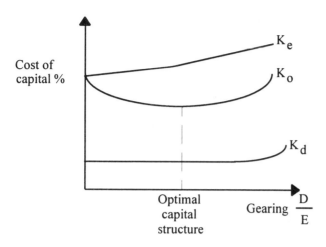

(c)   Modigliani and Miller proposition I (1958)

❑   All companies with the same earnings in the same risk class have the same future income stream and should therefore have the same value, independent of capital structure

(i)

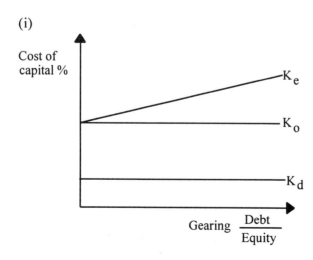

(ii)

Proposition I *Without tax*	Proposition II *With tax*

$$V_g = V_{ug} \qquad\qquad V_g = V_{ug} + Dt$$

$$k_{eg}=k_{eu}+\frac{D}{E}(k_{eu}\text{-}k_d) \qquad k_{eg}=k_{eu}+(1\text{-}t)\frac{D}{E}(k_{eu}\text{-}k_d)$$

$$WACC_g=WACC_u \qquad WACC_g=WACC_u(1\text{-}\frac{Dt}{D+E})$$

V   =   Value of firm (V_g = value of geared firm, V_u = value of ungeared firm)

k_e =   Cost of equity (k_{eg} = cost of equity in geared firm, k_{eu} = cost of equity in ungeared firm)

k_d =   Cost of debt (must be gross of tax)

D   =   MV of debt

E   =   MV of equity

t   =   Corporation tax rate

❑   The without tax formulae are simply a special case of the with tax formulae with $t = 0$

(iii)   Assumptions

❑   Investors are rational

❑   Investors have the same view of the future

❑   Personal and corporate gearing are perfect substitutes

❑   Information is freely available

❑   No transactions costs

❑   No tax

❑   Firms can be grouped into similar risk classes

The arbitrage 'proof', which incorporates these assumptions, can be used to support the M&M Proposition I.

(d)   Modigliani and Miller Proposition II (1963)

The values of companies with the same earnings in the same risk class are no longer independent. Companies with a higher gearing ratio have a greater net future income stream and therefore a higher value

(i)

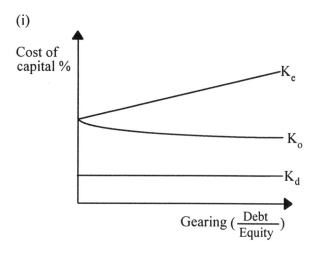

Gearing ($\frac{\text{Debt}}{\text{Equity}}$)

❑   As gearing increases, the WACC steadily decreases

(ii)   Theory - Arbitrage proof in a world with corporation taxes

Assume two companies, identical in every aspect expect G is financed by £1,000 of 10% irredeemable debt. Assumptions in (c) (iii) still hold apart from corporation tax is now 35%

The **traditional** view of the two companies could be

	U £	G £
EBIT	500	500
Interest	-	(100)
	500	400
Tax (35%)	(175)	(140)
Dividends	325	260
Cost of equity k_e	20%	26%
	£	£
Value of equity (E)	1,625	1,000
Value of debt (D)	-	1,000
Value of firm (V)	1,625	2,000
WACC	20%	16.25%

If an investor owned 10% of G's equity (Income £26) he should arbitrage ie,

- Sell his stake in G for £100

- Adopt the same financial risk as G by borrowing a proportional amount at 10% = £1,000 × 10% × (1 -0.35) = £65

- Buy 10% of U's equity for £162.50 to give the same income as before ie,

	£
Dividends from U	32.50
Interest on loan	(6.50)
Income	26.00

But: investor has spare funds (£100 + £65 - £162.50 = £2.50) which can be invested elsewhere to increase his income for the same level of risk

- Result - Market pressure will quickly compete away this 'money machine'. (G's equity will fall in price, U's equity will rise.) Assuming (for convenience) all the price changes are concentrated on G this will give an equilibrium value of equity of £975 (162.50 - 65 = £97.5 for 10%) and a value of the firm of £1,975 for G

(iii) Betas and gearing

- Betas are a way of measuring required rates of return and should respond to changes in gearing in the way predicted by M&M

- $$\beta_{asset} = \beta_e \frac{E}{E + D(1-t)} + \beta_d \frac{D(1-t)}{E + D(1-t)}$$

Normally β_d is assumed to be zero, so the above equation can be rewritten

$$\beta_{asset} = \beta \text{ equity ungeared}$$
$$= \beta \text{ equity geared} \times \frac{E}{E + D(1-t)}$$

- As based on theories of M&M, subject to the limitations of their theory

(iv)   Limitations of M&M Proposition II

$V_g = V_u + Dt$ -   Bankruptcy   -   Agency
costs (1)   costs (2)

-    Tax   -   Personal
exhaustion (3)   taxes (4)

(1)   Bankruptcy costs

The higher the level of gearing the greater the risk of bankruptcy with the associated costs of financial distress

$V_g = V_u + Dt$ -   Expected   present value of the costs of financial distress

(2)   Agency costs

Costs of restrictive covenants to protect the interests of debt holders at high levels of gearing

(3)   Taxation exhaustion

The value of the company will be reduced if advantage cannot be taken of the tax relief associated with debt interest

(4)   Personal taxes (Miller's critique 1977)

Investors will be concerned with returns net of all taxes

- If a firm's income is paid out as debt interest, corporation tax savings are made (see M&M 1963) but investors will have to pay income tax on debt interest

- If a firm's income is paid out as equity return, corporation tax has to be paid but personal tax is saved (via the imputation system as dividends or by avoidance of capital gains tax by delaying sale or using exemptions)

- In deciding its gearing level, a firm should consider its corporation tax position and the personal tax position of its investors if it wishes to maximise their wealth

❑ Firms will gear up until marginal investors face a personal tax cost of holding debt equal to the corporation tax saving. At this point there is no further advantage to gearing. Under current UK tax legislation this situation appears unlikely

Practical constraints on level of gearing

❑ General points

There are many practical constraints on the actual level of gearing

❑ Organisation's perception of its debt capacity, based on its potential ability to repay such debt

❑ View of providers of capital as to acceptable level of gearing. (This can dramatically change. Note the leveraged MBOs in late 1980s)

❑ Quality of asset backing to the debt

❑ Expected cash flows and risk attached

❑ Tax position of organisation

❑ Size of organisation

❑ Countries in which funds invested and borrowed

❑ Measurement of debt capacity

❑ Based on ability to repay

❑ Two main methods are

❑ Cash flow - 'free' cash flow available to repay borrowings over an acceptable period, under going concern circumstances

❑ Asset protection - the ability of assets in liquidation or forced sale (eg, special management or receivership) to generate enough cash to repay specifically identified debts

    ❑   A borrower will be concerned with cash flow, since his overriding interest will be only when the business is a going concern

    ❑   To a lender, asset protection may be either the main, or the subsidiary, element in defining debt capacity

7.5 Estimate the cost of capital for individual investments and divisions, including use of the 'pure play' method with ungearing and regearing beta

CAPM can be used to find a suitable discount rate for an individual investment/division, estimating the beta value of the investment by using the beta of a company in a similar area of business. However different companies can have different debt structures which affect their betas. M&M show how this problem can be solved by ungearing and then regearing the beta using the equation

$$\beta_g = \beta_u \left(1 + \frac{D(1-t)}{E} \right)$$

where
- β_g = beta equity for the geared company
- β_u = beta equity for the ungeared company
- D = market value of debt
- E = market value of equity
- t = corporation tax rate

Example

X plc manufactures TV sets. It is considering a more risky new project selling video games. X is currently ungeared and has an equity beta of 0.9. The average beta amongst video games sellers is 1.8, while their average gearing is 20% debt : 80% equity. Risk free investments yield 6%, the market return is 20% and corporation tax is 33%.

What required rate of return should X plc look for in its new project if it remains financed purely by equity?

Answer

We must first ungear the quoted beta for video games sellers.

$$1.8 = \beta_u \left(1 + \frac{20 \times (1 - 0.33)}{80} \right)$$

$$\beta_u = \frac{1.8}{1.1675} = 1.54$$

This beta represents the pure systematic risk of the video games industry, excluding any financial risk arising from gearing.

$$R_s \quad = \quad R_f + \beta\,(R_m - R_f)$$

$$= \quad 6 + 1.54\,(20 - 6)$$

$$= \quad 27.6\%$$

X plc requires a return of 27.6% from the new project.

Note that if X plc took on debt itself, a new geared beta for the company could be estimated from the geared beta equation used above.

7.6 Discuss the relevance of the cost of capital for unlisted companies and public sector organisations

Unlisted companies

❑   no external share price exists, so no cost of capital can be calculated or beta estimated.

❑   dividends are likely to be manipulated each year depending on shareholders' personal tax positions

❑   best method to estimate cost of capital is to take the cost of a similar listed company and add a risk premium

Public sector organisations

❑   the government sets a discount rate in real terms against which all large public sector projects are appraised.

❑   however there are significant non-financial costs and benefits from most public sector projects which must also be taken into account. This is usually done as part of a formal cost benefit analysis exercise.

7.7 Explain the practical problems of estimating an appropriate discount rate, and understand the margin of error that is involved in cost of capital estimates

The practical problems have been demonstrated above. A company's WACC can only be used directly to appraise new projects if

❑   the gearing ratio is unchanged by the project

❑   the project is of the same risk class as the whole company

Both of these assumptions are likely to be valid in the majority of cases.

Session 8   The Interaction of Investment and Financing Decisions

8.1   Understand the adjusted present value technique of investment appraisal including how to estimate the base case NPV and the financing side effects of an investment

    Step 1   Estimate the base case NPV assuming that the project is financed entirely by equity

    Step 2   Estimate the financial effect of the actual method of financing (eg, tax, issue costs etc)

    Step 3   Add the values from steps 1 and 2 to give the APV

If the APV is positive, accept the project

The APV method has the advantage of breaking down a complex problem into its constituent parts rather than trying to encapsulate the whole problem into determining a single discount rate.

8.2   Discuss the practical problems of using the APV technique

❑   relies on the M&M Proposition II formulae to be valid so requires the M&M assumptions to hold true

❑   different discount rates should be applied to the different side effects, which can become complicated

❑   the danger of getting bogged down in the detail, and not being able to see the wood from the trees

8.3   Discuss alternatives to the capital asset pricing model, including the Arbitrage Pricing Theory *(Note:* detailed knowledge is not required)

CAPM suffers from a number of problems, theoretical as well as practical, so researchers have sought other relations for the expected return on a share

❑   CAPM is a single index model

$$r_s = r_f + \beta\,(r_m - r_f)$$

where a security's expected return is a function of only one factor, the beta value.

❑   APT is a multi-index model

$$r_s = a + b_1 f_1 + b_2 f_2 + ...$$

where $a, b_1, b_2, ...$ are constants

                      $f_1, f_2, ...$ are the various factors which influence share returns

For example f_1 could be the return on the market (as in CAPM), f_2 could be an industry index, f_3 an interest rate index etc.

❑   Arbitrage profits exist when profits can be made at no risk at all eg, better returns are available from a different portfolio at the same level of risk.

APT states that when no further arbitrage profits are possible, the expected return from a security is given by:

$$r_s = r_f + \beta_1 (r_1 - r_f) + \beta_2 (r_2 - r_f) + ...$$

where r_f =   the risk free rate

        β_i =   constants expressing the security's sensitivity to each factor

        r_i =   the expected return on a portfolio with unit sensitivity to factor i and zero sensitivity to any other factor

The model was proposed by Ross in 1976 but has not yet been developed into anything of practical use. Further work is required to identify

❑   the factors affecting security prices

❑   methods of estimating r_f and the β_i.

Session 9   *Corporate Dividend Policy*

9.1   Describe the practical influences on dividend policy, including the possible effects of both corporate and personal taxation

Dividends in an imperfect market

(i)   Imperfect information

❑   Dividends are an important source of information

❑   Share price will increase if the dividend is greater than expected and vice versa

(ii)   Transactions costs

❑   Shareholder cannot costlessly replace a withheld dividend by selling shares

❑   Company will benefit by financing investments from retained earnings to avoid the high cost associated with raising new finance

(iii)   Preference for current income

❑   It is sometimes argued that shareholders prefer high dividend payouts as they see these as more secure than capital gains (the 'bird in the hand' theory)

❑   This argument is however weak. Current dividends are safe, but so are current capital gains. Future dividends are just as uncertain as future capital gains

(iv)   Distorting taxes

❑   Individuals will generally prefer dividends to capital gains whether a basic-rate or higher-rate tax payer, subject to the complications

  ❑   Exemption limit for capital gains

  ❑   Non-tax paying individuals

  ❑   Tax-exempt institutions

❑   Companies with a surplus ACT position would rather pay low dividends to mitigate the problem

9.2 Discuss the role of dividends as signals of future prospects

Companies will try to offer a constant growth in dividends each year, regardless of the volatility of their earnings. An increased dividend above the level expected by the market from previous signals indicates good prospects, and the share price will be marked up accordingly. A reduced dividend below the expected level will depress the share price.

9.3 Discuss the alternative arguments with respect to the effect of dividend policy on share prices

Modigliani and Miller's dividend irrelevance hypothesis

(i)   Theory

Given a set investment policy, proponents of the dividend irrelevance hypothesis claim that dividends themselves are not irrelevant, but the pattern of payments ie, the split between retentions and dividends, is irrelevant

The shareholder will be indifferent to the dividend policy provided the present value of dividend payments remains unchanged

(ii)   Assumptions

❑   A set investment policy so that shareholders know the reason for withholding dividends

❑   No transactions costs

❑   No distorting taxes

❑   Share prices move in the manner predicted by the model

As a result the shareholder can maintain his level of income in the case of a withheld dividend by selling shares to generate 'home made' dividends, with no consequent decrease in wealth

Practical approaches to dividend policy

(i)   Stable policy with moderate payout

❑   Stable level of dividends or constant growth to avoid sharp movements in share price

❑   Moderate payout policy in order to sustain the level of dividends in the face of fluctuating earnings

❑　　　Very common approach for quoted companies

(ii)　　Constant payout ratio

❑　　　Constant proportion of earnings paid out as dividend

❑　　　Not particularly suitable as dividends will fluctuate

(iii)　Residual dividend policy

❑　　　Remaining earnings, after funding all profitable projects, are paid out as dividend

❑　　　A rational approach, saves transaction costs

❑　　　Tends to lead to fluctuating dividends and therefore not particularly suitable

(iv)　Clientele theory

❑　　　Consistent dividend policy is maintained which will attract a group of shareholders to whom the policy is suited in terms of tax, need for current income etc

(v)　　Other considerations

❑　　　Legality, re distributable profits

❑　　　Existence of inflation and consideration of real profitability

❑　　　Growth and requirements for retained earnings

❑　　　Liquidity position

❑　　　Availability of funds (small companies)

❑　　　Stability of earnings

Session 10   Business Planning

10.1   Review the nature of financial control - the three levels of control: strategic, tactical and operational

Strategic control	ROCE, RI, gearing levels
Tactical control	pricing decisions, cash flow forecasts
Operational control	budgets, variance analysis

10.2   Discuss the information requirements for financial control, forecasts, decision support and monitoring

- ❏   definition of control

- ❏   budget variances

- ❏   sales variances

- ❏   variance analysis

You will have met the control process in your earlier studies and will appreciate the three aspects of

- ❏   setting standards as performance guidelines

- ❏   measuring actual performance

- ❏   comparing the two and taking corrective action if required

10.3   Understand the information needs of short-term financial planning

- ❏   projected profit and loss account

- ❏   projected cash flow statement

- ❏   projected balance sheet

- ❏   statement of relevant assumptions

- ❏   statement of contingency plans

- ❏   financing implications

- ❏   methods of control

A short-term plan would generally be prepared for the forthcoming one year period, broken down if required into months or quarters. The cash flow statement, in particular, would normally be prepared on a month-by-month basis.

10.4   Explain how budgeting, monitoring and controlling cash flows, including pricing, raising finance, repaying debt etc, may be used to meet short and medium term financial objectives

The control of cash flows is of key interest to the financial manager, because the forecast financing requirement must be satisfied. The manager can take early steps to research potential sources of new finance before a crisis emerges.

10.5   Understand how business plans are developed and analysed to meet specified objectives

Business plans set out how to achieve specific financial objectives. The plan covers a number of years (3 to 5 typically, but could be longer) and is part of the company's overall strategic plan.

The plan is developed from forecasts:

❑   environmental forecasts

❑   industry forecasts

❑   forecasts for the company itself

10.6   Analyse past, current and expected future performance of the organisation through ratios and other techniques to provide relevant information for business planning

(a)   Use of ratios

❑   Ratios of particular relevance when the performance of the profit centre and its constituent parts is measured by comparison with other organisations or parts of the profit centre

❑   Evaluation of the organisation as a whole

Ratios can be calculated from data produced by the accounting information system. Ratios can be used

▫   To compare results over a period of time

▫   To measure performance against other organisations

❑   To compare results with a target

Key ratio used in practice is return on capital employed (ROCE)

❑   Evaluation of parts of the organisation

    ❑   If the accounting information system can break down parts of the organisation as investment centres all the ratios used for evaluation of the performance of the organisation can be computed and can be used in the same ways

    ❑   ROCE tends to be termed return on investment (ROI)

    ❑   Other ratios required for non-investment centres

(b)   Structures of operating ratios - the pyramid

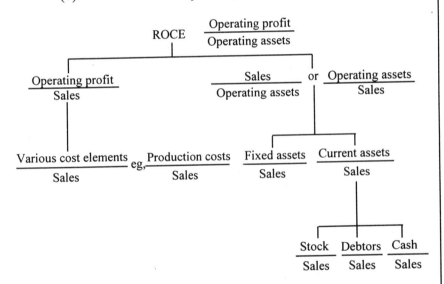

Short term liquidity

❑   Current/working capital ratio

    ❑ $\dfrac{\text{Current assets}}{\text{Current liabilities}}$

    ❑   Norm 2:1 but industry variation

    ❑   Low ratio may = insolvency

    ❑   High ratio may = not maximising return on working capital

    ❑   Can be manipulated by window dressing

❑ Liquidity, acid test or quick ratio

    ❑ $$\frac{\text{Debtors} + \text{current asset investments} + \text{cash}}{\text{Short term creditors}}$$

    ❑ Measures more immediate position (ie, excludes stock)

    ❑ Norm 1 : 1 but industry specific

    ❑ Can be manipulated by window dressing

❑ Gearing

    ❑ $$\frac{\text{Fixed return capital}}{\text{Equity capital and reserves} + \text{Fixed return capital}}$$

    ❑ Denominator could be computed on assets side of B/S:

    Total assets less current liabilities

    ❑ Highly geared company

        ❑ Substantial proportion of capital is preference shares, debentures or loan stock

        ❑ Share price often more volatile

        ❑ Must have

            ❑ Stable profits

            ❑ Suitable assets for security eg, property investment, hotel industry

    ❑ Limitations

        ❑ Distorted by different accounting policies eg, treatment of goodwill, revaluing assets

        ❑ Non-recording of assets eg, operating leases

❑ Ratios using free cash flow

    ❑ Definition

    Free cash flow = Revenues − costs − investment

    ❑ Example ratio

    Dividend cover in cash terms $= \dfrac{\text{Free cash flow}}{\text{Dividends paid}}$

□ Better than earnings-based ratios, since dividends are paid in cash. Cash-based ratios have become more popular in recent years with the increasing emphasis on cash management (eg, SSAP 10 scrapped in favour of FRS 1).

10.7 Compare actual and expected performance, highlighting areas for further investigation

Types of analysis

❑ Horizontal analysis 'line by line' analysis of current year with previous year(s)

Example

	19X3 £m	19X4 £m	% change
Turnover	951.9	1,156.5	+ 21.5
Cost of sales	617.1	739.0	+ 19.8

❑ Vertical analysis

□ Each balance sheet item is expressed as a percentage of the balance sheet total

□ Each profit and loss account item is expressed as a percentage of sales (or earnings)

Example

	19X3 £m	19X4 £m	Common size statements 19X3 %	19X4 %
Fixed assets				
Land and buildings	156.9	169.0	32.2	30.4
Plant and machinery	202.8	239.5	41.6	43.2
	359.7	408.5	73.8	73.6
Current assets				
Stocks, debtors	305.0	344.0	62.5	62.0
Other creditors (due within 1 year)	(163.5)	(181.6)	(33.5)	(32.7)
Creditors (due over 1 year	(13.5)	(16.0)	(2.8)	(2.9)
	487.7	554.9	100.0	100.0

❑ other techniques

□ standard variance analysis

□ product life cycle analysis

□ learning curve analysis

Session 11   Long-Term Planning

11.1   Understand the relationship between short-term and long-term financial planning, and the potential conflict between short term and long term objectives

❑   Long-term financial planning depends on

  ❑   corporate philosophy and mission statement

  ❑   meeting the shareholders' required rate of return

  ❑   'what if' analysis on spreadsheets

  ❑   gap analysis

❑   The planning exercise continues via

  ❑   strategic plans

  ❑   tactical plans

  ❑   operational plans

  ❑   monitoring deviations of actuals from operational plans

❑   Companies are often accused of favouring short-term profitability at the expense of long-term prosperity. Some of the reasons are

  ❑   reward systems

  ❑   fear of disappointing the markets

  ❑   fear of take-over

  ❑   dominance of accountants (perhaps) in UK industry

11.2   Describe top down versus bottom up planning systems

Top down

Senior management announce instructions which filter their way down through the organisation structure.

Bottom up

Information is gathered from lower levels, which is consolidated until a summary is produced for the board.

Long-term strategic decisions are ultimately the responsibility of senior management. They cannot shirk this role.

11.3   Understand the use of budgets to influence the success of financial planning

❑   long-term plans are implemented by developing them into a series of shorter term plans or budgets

❑   definition of budgets

You will have studied budgetary control in previous examinations.

11.4   Discuss the relationship of investment decisions to long term planning

❑   Types of investment decision

❑   internal investments

❑   external investments

❑   divestments

If the long term planning objective is to maximise the wealth of shareholders, then conventional DCF analysis can be applied to investment decisions.

11.5   Describe alternative strategies for long-term growth, organic growth versus external growth, and the key dimensions of strategy that need to be addressed if a business is considering organic growth

❑   conservative growth or high growth
     high growth is achieved by rapid diversification into similar markets as well as completely new markets

❑   horizontal diversification

❑   vertical diversification (backwards and forwards)

❑   concentric diversification

❑   conglomerate diversification

❑   the search for synergy $(2 + 2 = 5)$

The pros and cons of acquisition as a means of rapid growth are covered in the next session.

Session 12   Mergers and Acquisitions

12.1   Understand the arguments for and against mergers and acquisitions

❑   horizontal mergers

❑   vertical mergers (backwards or forwards)

❑   conglomerate mergers

❑   a merger is rational if synergy is created

An expansion policy based on merger or take-over can be justified on the basis of synergy ie,

Value of A plc and B plc combined	>	Value of A plc operating independently	+	Value of B plc operating independently

(sometimes stated as 2 + 2 = 5)

❑   Possible sources of synergy   √   =   sensible argument
                                     x   =   silly argument

   ❑   Operating economies

      √   Economies of scale
      √   Economies of vertical integration
      √   Complementary resources
      √   Elimination of inefficiency
      √   Surplus managerial talent
      √   Surplus cash

   ❑   Market power

      √   The desire to earn monopoly profits (good for shareholders but not for public interest)

   ❑   Financial effects

      x   Diversification reduces risk (it only reduces total risk not systematic risk for well diversified shareholders)

      √   Diversification reduces variance of operating cash flows giving less bankruptcy risk and therefore cheaper borrowing

      x   High PE ratio companies can impose their multiples on low PE ratio companies (Bootstrapping)

- ❏ Conclusion of synergy

  - ❑ Synergy is not automatic

  - ❑ When bid premiums are considered the only consistent winners in mergers and take-overs are victim company shareholders

12.2 Contrast merger and acquisition activity in the UK and USA with activity in continental Europe and Japan, and discuss the implications of the differences that exist for corporate governance.

Merger activity is much higher in the UK and USA than in Germany or Japan. This is principally because banks dominate the financial systems of Germany and Japan, and develop long-term relationships with the companies they serve, taking significant equity stakes. They would not sell these stakes to a predator.

In the UK and USA institutional shareholders are willing to sell if offered a significant premium.

SSAP 22 permits goodwill to be offset directly against reserves, which is often stated as encouraging UK take-overs.

12.3 Describe the alternative strategies and tactics of mergers and acquisitions

- ❏ Strategy

  - ❑ identify a likely acquisition target

  - ❑ approach the board in confidence to gauge their reaction

  - ❑ decide on a price to offer

  - ❑ decide on the terms of the offer

- ❏ Tactics

  - ❑ dawn raid

  - ❑ make a general offer

12.4 Discuss how possible acquisition targets may be identified using financial or other information

- ❏ research targets' turnover and market share

- ❏ poor cost control

- ❏ seeking dynamic management

- ❑ existing spread of shareholdings

- ❑ trade magazines

- ❑ published accounts/Extel cards

12.5 Estimate the value of potential target companies

Methods of valuing companies

- ❑ Earnings based

	Advantages	*Disadvantages*
Present value of future cash flows	- Theoretically sound	- Estimation of future costs and suitable discount rate - Only suitable for controlling interest
PE Ratio	- Simple - Few data requirements - Can be used for non-controlling interest	- Estimation of maintainable earnings - Estimation of suitable PE ratio (size, industry, systematic risk) - Adjustments for non marketability
Dividend valuation	- Simple - Can be used for non-controlling interest	- Estimating future dividends - Estimation of suitable cost of equity interest - Adjustments for non marketability

❑   Asset based

Historical cost	- Readily available	- Gives unexpired cost not value
Replacement cost	- Gives cost of setting up equivalent	- Excludes goodwill - Valuation problems - Only suitable for controlling interest
Net realisable value	- Gives disposal value to existing owners, often seen as a minimum figure	- Excludes goodwill - Valuation problems

❑   If the market value is available this should be seen as a minimum value.

12.6   Distinguish between the various methods of financing mergers and acquisitions - cash, debt, equity and hybrids, and assess the attractiveness of different financing alternatives to vendors.

	Advantages	*Disadvantages*
Cash	- Simple - Price certain	- Liquidity problems - Capital gains tax
Shares	- Saves cash - Maintains ownership state - Avoids capital gains tax	- Value uncertain - Dilution of EPS
Loan stock	- Saves cash - Avoids capital gains tax	- Gearing problems - Changes character of investment
Convertible loan stock	- Saves cash - Avoids capital gains tax - Target shareholders can continue on equity interest	- Gearing problems - Changes character of investment

12.7   Evaluate the various defences against take-overs, and be aware of any restrictions on their use as specified by the City Code

❑   Pre-offer defences

  ❑   poison pills
  ❑   keep dividends high
  ❑   regular revaluation of assets
  ❑   special terms in managers' service contracts

❑   Post-offer defences

  ❑   Argue that victim shares are undervalued, bidders' shares are overvalued (contrary to EMH but you may have inside information)

  ❑   Disclose favourable information

  ❑   Merge with a more friendly party (white knight defence)

  ❑   Appeal to Monopolies and Mergers Commission

  ❑   Reverse take-over

  ❑   Criticise the rationale claimed for the merger

All defence strategies must comply with the City Code

12.8   Identify key issues that influence the success of acquisitions, and recommend appropriate actions for a given situation

❑   price paid
❑   whether synergistic hopes turn out as expected
❑   motivation of employees
❑   compatibility of information systems
❑   future resource needs

12.9   Understand the importance of post-audit and monitoring of post-acquisition success

❑   too often management's attention turns to planning the next acquisition

❑   Drucker's 5 rules

❑   the 'human factor' is particularly important.

Session 13   *Financial Restructuring Alternatives And Decisions*

13.1   Describe the nature of, and reasons for, divestments

❑   Definition

Divestment is the withdrawal of investment in an activity.

Either the business is sold as a going concern **or** the assets associated with the activity are sold piecemeal

❑   Possible reasons for divestment

❑   earning inadequate return
❑   not a core activity
❑   risk too high
❑   need for cash

13.2   Describe 'unbundling' and 'demerging' of quoted companies

After a period of acquisition activity, a company may find that it has bought several large groups of businesses, some related to its chosen core activities but some connected with non-core activities. Unbundling is the process of selling off incidental businesses to release funds, reduce gearing and allow management to concentrate on their chosen core businesses.

A demerger is the opposite of a merger. A group is split into two or more separate parts of roughly comparable size which are large enough to carry on independently after the split eg, ICI and Zeneca.

13.3   Discuss the advantages of buy-outs, and understand the issues that a management team should address in the preparation of a buy-out proposal

❑   Distinguishing features

❑   Group of managers acquire effective control and substantial ownership of an operation and form an independent business

❑   Also employee buyouts, buyins, spinouts

❑   Motivations

❑   For sale   -   Parent company disposals due to losses, lack of fit, or size

-    Private business owners wishing to sell out

  ❑ For purchase - Potential high returns

       - Relatively low risk as compared to 'greenfield' starts

       - Elimination of managerial slack

       - Protects their jobs

 ❑ Issues to be addressed

   ❑ do the current owners wish to sell?
   ❑ will management top other bidders?
   ❑ business plan
   ❑ loss of group services
   ❑ clear management structure
   ❑ method of financing the deal

13.4 Identify situations in which a management buy-out is likely to offer the best value for a disposer

 ❑ there are few other potential purchasers

 ❑ the management have a plan to realise the company's potential

 ❑ the disposer could continue to offer central support services for a price

 ❑ the management have put together a financing package which does not need help from the disposer

13.5 Evaluate alternative sources of finance for buy-outs

 ❑ Commonly highly geared to leave managers with controlling interest in equity

 ❑ Support from institutions normally required

   ❑ Examples include clearing banks, 3i group, EIS funds etc. Syndication is common

   ❑ Institutions normally require business plans, details of exit routes, sometimes board representation

   ❑ Common instruments include debt, preference shares, equity (limited), mezzanine finance

 ❑ Other sources of finance

   ❑ leasing and hire purchase

> ❑ government grants eg, from area development agencies
>
> ❑ employees' pension scheme

13.6 Assess the viability of buy-outs from the viewpoint of both the buy-out team and the financial backers

❑ why do current owners wish to sell?

❑ does the proposed management team cover all key functions? If not, new appointments should be made

❑ business plan, particularly cash flow projections

❑ proposed sale price

❑ financing method

13.7 Identify the advantages and disadvantages of management buy-ins

Definition

A management buy-in is when a group of outside managers buys a controlling stake in a business.

❑ best when current management are not up to the job

❑ employee resistance can be experienced when the new management try to impose new ways of doing things

13.8 Identify and justify when a capital reconstruction may be required or appropriate

❑ s135 CA85: restructuring scheme

❑ s425 CA85: scheme of arrangement

13.9 Be aware of the importance of taking into account the interests of the various suppliers of capital in a reconstruction scheme

❑ ordinary shareholders have the prospect of future dividends

❑ preference shareholders may have to forgo arrears of their dividends, so offer them a higher coupon in future

❑ secured creditors could be offered free equity to persuade them not to apply for the company to be wound up

❑   unsecured creditors have the prospect of being paid in full

It is possible to devise a scheme such that every supplier of capital is better off after the scheme than before it. If this is not the case, then that class of capital provider will vote against the scheme and the court may not approve it.

13.10   Formulate a feasible reconstruction from given information

Method of scheme

❑   Write off P&L debit balance

❑   Write off fictitious assets, formation expenses, deferred expenditure

❑   Revalue other assets

❑   Reorganise capital structure

❑   Allow new capital to be raised

Guidelines for devising a scheme

❑   Capital reduction/reconstruction account allows write offs of assets to be matched by write offs of share capital

❑   Ordinary shareholders bear most of the write offs

Session 14 *Economic Influences On International Financial Management Decisions*

14.1 **Understand the nature, size and significance of multinational companies in the world economy**

❑ multinational companies (MNCs) are companies that own or control subsidiaries based in a number of overseas countries

❑ they engage in foreign direct investment ie, buying overseas factories, machinery etc, rather than just owning shares in overseas companies without contributing to their day-to-day management

❑ generally accepted definition is that a company must derive at least 25% of its annual sales from outside its home country before being recognised as an MNC

❑ horizontal integration

❑ vertical integration

❑ examples

   ❑ General Motors
   ❑ Royal Dutch Shell Group
   ❑ IBM

❑ large MNCs have annual turnovers greater than the GNPs of all but the largest countries

❑ many countries welcome MNCs to their shores hoping that they will bring jobs and economic activity

❑ however conflicts can arise between the MNC's desire to maximise profits and the host country's desire to develop economy

14.2 **Discuss the influence of exchange rates, international capital markets and changes in global competition patterns on the strategies of multinational companies, with particular reference to the EC, USA and Japan**

❑ originally MNC activity was US-driven after WWII to rebuild Europe

❑ US focus then shifted to Canada and Latin America

❑ European MNCs began to emerge in the 1950s

   ❑ UK: BP
   ❑ Italy: Fiat
   ❑ Germany: Daimler-Benz

❑　　product specialisation and process specialisation

❑　　Japanese MNCs emerged in the 1960s

　　　❑　　Nissan, Hitachi, etc

　　　❑　　located in newly industrialised countries (NICs)

　　　❑　　located in Europe to gain access to EC markets.

14.3　Understand the theory and practice of free trade, and the problems of protectionism, through tariff and non-tariff barriers

❑　　possibility of economies of scale, division of labour

❑　　Adam Smith: theory of absolute advantage

❑　　Ricardo: theory of comparative advantage

❑　　factor endowments theory

❑　　relevance of product life cycle theory

Methods of protectionism

❑　　tariffs
❑　　quotas
❑　　voluntary export limits
❑　　excessive red tape
❑　　exchange controls
❑　　operation of cartels

Protectionism aims at boosting economic wealth in the home country, but retaliatory measures often defeat its purpose.

14.4　Describe the major trade agreements and customs unions (the European Community, North American Free Trade Area, EFTA etc)

❑　　The European Community

　　　❑　　called the European Union since November 1993

　　　❑　　EEC originally established with 6 members in 1958

　　　❑　　EU currently 15 members

　　　❑　　single market created from 1 January 1993

　　　❑　　two thirds of EU budget spent on CAP

    ❑   Maastricht treaty a further step towards economic integration

❑   North American Free Trade Area (NAFTA)

    ❑   Comprises Canada, the USA and Mexico

    ❑   established in 1993 as a free trading bloc throughout the area

❑   European Free Trade Area (EFTA)

    ❑   established in 1960 to promote free trade in Europe to counter the EEC which was working towards economic (and political) integration.

    ❑   In 1973 the UK and Denmark left EFTA to join the EEC

    ❑   EFTA linked up with the EC in 1993 to create the European Economic Area (EEA) matching NAFTA in size

    ❑   The remaining EFTA member countries may join the EC in the future, leaving EFTA with no separate role.

14.5   Understand the nature and significance of the balance of payments and the possible effects of national balance of payments problems on the financial decisions of companies

    ❑   the balance of payments is a statistical record of a country's international trade transactions (current account) and capital transactions with the rest of the world over a period of time

Example

UK balance of payments 1992

	£bn
Current account	
Exports	107
Imports	(121)
Visible balance	(14)
Invisibles balance	2
	(12)
UK external assets and liabilities: net transactions	2
Balancing item	10
	12

❑ temporary problems can be financed by short-term borrowing

❑ longer term problems can be treated by

  ❑ devaluing the currency

  ❑ raising interest rates

  ❑ tight fiscal and monetary policies

  ❑ imposing tariffs and other forms of protectionism

14.6 Explain the objectives and function of GATT, and describe the major rounds of GATT and their achievements

❑ GATT began in 1947 with 23 member countries with the aim of promoting free trade throughout the world

❑ there are now more than 100 member countries, including many newly industrialised countries

❑ the objectives of GATT are

  ❑ to reduce barriers to free trade
  ❑ to eliminate discrimination from world trade
  ❑ to encourage consultation before protectionist measures are imposed

❑ the MFN (most favoured nation) principle

❑ GATT talks over the years take place in a series of 'rounds' of negotiation

  ❑ the Kennedy round (1962-7) achieved large cuts in tariffs

  ❑ the Tokyo round (1973-9) led to further tariff reductions

  ❑ the Uruguay round ended in December 1993, after major problems between the USA and the EC in reducing CAP subsidies had finally been settled.

❑ future in the hands of the newly-formed World Trade Organisation (WTO)

Session 15   *The International Financial System*

15.1   Understand the role of the major international financial institutions, including the IMF, the Bank for International Settlements and the International Bank for Reconstruction and Development (The World Bank)

❑   IMF

   ❑   founded in 1944 at the Bretton Woods conference

   ❑   aims to promote world trade and maintain world monetary stability

   ❑   150 member countries

   ❑   helps countries with balance of payments deficits by making loans in the form of Special Drawing Rights (SDRs)

   ❑   loans are often dependent on stringent internal economic adjustments designed to assist countries rebalance their budgets

❑   BIS

   ❑   founded in 1930, based in Switzerland, the supervisory body for central banks

   ❑   assists central bankers in investing monetary assets

   ❑   acts as trustee for the IMF in loans to developing countries

   ❑   promotes capital adequacy of banks by publishing risk-based capital standards, formulated originally in 1988

❑   World Bank

   ❑   founded in 1944 at the Bretton Woods conference

   ❑   initial aim to finance the reconstruction of Europe following WWII

   ❑   now provides developing countries with long-term low interest credit for industrial development when private finance is not available

       ❑   financed by the Bank issuing its own bonds, traded in the capital markets of developed countries

15.2 Understand the workings of international money markets

❑ International banking has resulted in massive:

       ❑   cross-border lending, and
       ❑   cross-currency lending

❑ Three categories of international banking:

       ❑   multinational banking
       ❑   wholesale banking
       ❑   offshore banking

15.3 Outline the major factors affecting the development of international banking

❑ The recent growth in international banking can be explained by:

       ❑   deregulation offering new profit opportunities
       ❑   natural growth
       ❑   cross-hauling
       ❑   lower costs arising from technological advances
       ❑   desire to diversify to reduce systematic risk

15.4 Understand the role of international banks in international finance, including international bank lending through syndication and multi-option facilities and other means

❑ You must appreciate the importance of

       ❑   correspondent banking, involving letters of credit/promissory notes
       ❑   representative offices
       ❑   overseas branches
       ❑   overseas subsidiaries

❑ In banking parlance, syndication refers to a group lending whereby a group of bankers each agrees to advance a portion of the funding.

❑ Multi-option facilities allow companies to choose how to raise funds from a number of funding instruments. Examples are

       ❑   note issuance facilities (NIFs)
       ❑   standby note issuance facilities (SNIFs)
       ❑   revolving underwriting facilities (RUFs)

15.5 **Describe the nature and development of the Euromarkets, including the Eurocurrency, Eurobond and Euroequity markets**

The Euromarket refers to transactions between banks and the depositors/borrowers of Eurocurrency. Eurocurrency refers to currency held on deposit in banks outside its home country eg, Eurodollars are US $ in a bank account outside the US

Eurobonds are bonds denominated in a currency other than that of the country in which they are issued.

The Euroequity market refers to the international equity market where shares in US corporations, say, are traded in London and Paris.

Note also Euronotes and Eurocommercial paper.

15.6 **Explain the types of financing instruments that are available to corporate treasurers on the Euromarkets, for both borrowing and financial investment.**

❑ Eurocurrency deposits: either fixed term or tradable CD

❑ Eurocurrency loans: term can vary from overnight to medium-term

❑ Eurobonds: medium term, interest paid gross

❑ Euronotes: short-term unsecured promissory notes

15.7 **Understand the role of domestic capital markets, especially stock exchanges, in financing the activities of multinational companies.**

❑ primary market: corporations raise money

❑ secondary market: second hand market for investors

❑ London market uses the SEAQ computerised price quotation system. Transactions are executed by telephone between buyer and seller.

❑ multinationals tend to list their capital on several international markets to maximise the liquidity of trading in their stocks.

15.8 **Understand the nature of the global debt problem**

❑ less developed countries (LDCs) can be split between

❑ low income LDCs eg, Central Africa. Their debt tends to be to development agencies such as the IMF and World Bank

- ❑ middle income LDCs eg, Latin America. Their debt tends to be to private commercial banks.

❑ commercial banks fear a default could destabilise the entire world banking system.

❑ the problem arose when OPEC countries in the 1970s invested their large current account surpluses with Western banks, who lent them on to LDCs, believing that the default risk was low since governments could not go bust.

❑ the oil price rise in 1979 fuelled inflation, which Western governments sought to combat by raising interest rates. This in turn pushed the developed countries into recession.

❑ the twin effects of higher interest rates and lower export prospects due to the recession put LDCs in a position where they could no longer service their debt.

❑ the situation is less serious now after a programme of debt forgiveness and rescheduling, and IMF-imposed changes in LDCs' domestic economic management.

Session 16   Foreign Trade

16.1   Advise clients on the alternative methods of exporting and importing

This is assumed to refer to the alternative methods of **financing** exports and imports.

❑   Traditional sources

  ❑   bank overdrafts
  ❑   acceptance credit lines
  ❑   produce loans
  ❑   bills of exchange
  ❑   promissory notes

❑   Non-traditional sources

  ❑   factoring
  ❑   forfaiting
  ❑   leasing and hire purchase

16.2   Understand the risks of foreign trade, currency, credit/commercial and political

❑   currency risks can be managed by

  ❑   internal techniques (leading and lagging, netting etc)

  ❑   external techniques (forwards, futures and options etc)

❑   credit risk
❑   trade risk
❑   liquidity risk
❑   political risk
❑   physical risk

16.3   Explain the advantage and disadvantages of using documentary letters of credit, bills of exchange, acceptances etc, in foreign trade

❑   documentary letters of credit

  ❑   guarantees payment to the exporter, backed by banks

  ❑   the exporter gains comfort from the fact that the importer's untested intention to pay is guaranteed by a secure bank, subject to the documents being presented correctly

> ❑ irrevocable letters of credit provide the greatest security

❑ Bills of exchange

> ❑ drawn up by the exporter and despatched with the goods to the importer
>
> ❑ once signed by the importer, the importer has agreed to pay on demand, or on a fixed or determinable future date
>
> ❑ term bills can be discounted (ie, sold) by the exporter providing immediate funds

❑ Acceptance credits

> ❑ method of short-term finance for exporters
>
> ❑ costs are generally lower than bank overdrafts

Note also that an exporter could avoid the above complications by insisting that all payments are received in advance.

16.4 Describe the insurance that is available to protect against the risks of foreign trade

❑ ECGD

> ❑ short-term cover privatised and now run by NCM UK
>
> ❑ greater than 180 days cover run by the project group of ECGD
>
> ❑ provides cover against political risk rather than currency risk

❑ UK exporters can arrange Supplier Credit Finance

❑ overseas importers of UK exports can arrange Buyer Credit Finance

16.5 Describe and evaluate the sources of finance for foreign trade, including forfaiting and international factoring

❑ Forfaiting

> ❑ source of medium-term export finance
>
> ❑ bank discounts overseas trade bills for an exporter but forgoes the right of recourse to the exporter (the bank forfeits its rights, hence the name)

- ❑ exporter obtains benefit of immediate liquidity, but can be expensive

❑ Factoring

- ❑ a factoring company (often a subsidiary of a bank) buys trade debt from an exporter for cash, charging a commission on the sale

- ❑ other services can also be provided such as running the sales ledger, credit insurance etc, also at a cost

- ❑ allows exporters to offer open account terms to customers, while credit risk is controlled

- ❑ provides an additional (though sometimes expensive) source of finance when liquidity is stretched.

16.6 Describe the main features of countertrade, and various alternatives that exist for foreign trade deals other than for monetary payments

- ❑ countertrade is an agreement where exports to a country only occur on the condition that the exporter in turn buys imports from the same country in return

- ❑ usually occurs because the importing company lacks foreign exchange reserves eg, Russia paying companies in oil in recent years

- ❑ various forms

    - ❑ barter
    - ❑ counter purchase
    - ❑ buy back
    - ❑ switch accounts

Session 17   Exchange Rate Systems

17.1   Describe the major developments in exchange rate systems since Bretton Woods, including the European Monetary System and the ERM

❑   Bretton Woods conference in 1944 established a pegged exchange rate system. Countries exchange rates were permitted to vary up to 1% either side of their declared par rate. Effectively a fixed exchange rate system with rare alterations in par rates.

❑   1967 devaluation of the pound from $2.80 to $2.40.

❑   1972 UK government abandoned fixed rates for the pound and let sterling float.

❑   1979 EMS established to co-ordinate EC economic policies.

□   ECU created as a basket of EC currencies

□   European Monetary Co-operation Fund provides loans to help maintain currencies within agreed ERM bands

□   ERM a pegged exchange rate system for member countries who wish to join

❑   1990 UK agrees to join the ERM, allowed a 6% divergence band for sterling, compared with 2.25% for most other currencies

❑   1992 UK leaves the ERM. Massive speculation by currency traders of an imminent devaluation had led to an unsustainable position within the mechanism

❑   1993 Further action by speculators led to the effective abandonment of the whole ERM system, with most divergence bands expanded to 15%, and the prospects for a common currency thrown into question.

17.2   Explain the workings of the foreign exchange markets, types of quotation, spot and forward rates

❑   spot foreign exchange market

□   the exchange of currencies at the current rate of exchange

□   delivery immediate (ie, next day)

❑   forward foreign exchange market

    ❑   contract to exchange currencies at a rate determined today

    ❑   delivery at a specified future date (eg, in 3 months)

    ❑   rate determined by forces of supply and demand for future money

17.3   The determinants of exchange rates

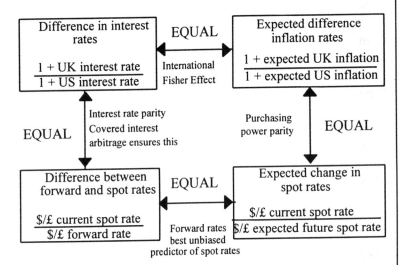

Identifying and protecting against price risk

Reading quotes

	US $/£
Spot	1.7053 - 1.7089
3 months forward	2.5 - 3.5 cents discount

❑   Dealer always wins. If we wished to convert £ to $ we would receive $1.7053. Converting $ to £ would cost $1.7089 per £

❑   Outright forward rates are

	US $/£	
Spot	1.7053	1.7089
Add on discount	0.0250	0.0350 (ADDIS!)
Forward rate	1.7303	1.7439 (SPREAD)
		INCREASES)

❏ Cross rates

Spot	FF/$	7.5004	-	7.6003
Spot	$/£	1.7053	-	1.7089

What is FF/£ spot rate?

£1 buys $1.7053, buys $1.7053 \times 7.5004 = $ FF 12.7904

hence Spot FF/£   12.7904 - 12.9882

❏ Option date contracts

Forward contracts with variable exercise dates. Normally priced at least favourable forward rate in period concerned.

71

Session 18   *Currency Risk*

18.1   **Discuss the types of currency risk - transaction, translation and economic exposure, and their importance to companies**

❑   transaction exposure   -   transactions on credit are denominated in a foreign currency

❑   translation exposure   -   arises when overseas financial statements are translated into sterling in accordance with SSAP 20

❑   economic exposure   -   arises when the present value of future cash flows changes due to a change in exchange rates

18.2   **Evaluate alternative strategies that companies might adopt with respect to currency exposure**

Covering transaction exposure

❑   Cover in forward market = buy or sell appropriate currency forward

❑   Cover in money market

	UK Importer		*UK Exporter*
❑	Borrow in sterling	❑	Borrow in foreign currency
❑	Convert to foreign currency spot	❑	Convert to sterling spot
❑	Invest in foreign currency so that proceeds pay foreign supplier	❑	Invest in UK and repay foreign loan with customer receipt

18.3   **Discuss and evaluate traditional methods of currency risk management, including currency of invoice, leading and lagging, netting, matching, and internal asset and liability management**

❑   Lead or lag = pay early or late to avoid unfavourable currency movements.   Settlement discounts may be involved

❑   Netting - offset debtors and creditors in same currency and only cover the net position

❑   Invoice in £ - commercial problems

❑   Do nothing = speculation

In the long run doing nothing should give the same results as covering (forward rates are an unbiased predictor of spot rates).

❑   Matching - the use of receipts in a particular currency to meet payment obligations in the same currency

❑   Internal asset and liability management - choose the currencies in which the assets and liabilities of a company are denominated. Assets should be in strong currencies and liabilities in weak currencies.

18.4   **Evaluate hedging strategies using forward foreign exchange contracts**

Example

A company might expect to receive DM 100,000 in six months time. If it does nothing the company is exposed to the risk of the DM strengthening over the period and so the company would receive fewer pounds at the end of the period.

❑   Strategy using the spot market

      ❑   borrow DM 100,000

      ❑   sell the DM in the spot market for £ to eliminate the exchange risk

      ❑   use the receipt in 6 months time to pay off the loan

❑   Strategy using the forward market

      ❑   enter into a forward contract to sell DM 100,000 in 6 months time

Session 19   *Risk Management*

19.1   **Outline the recent volatility of interest rates and exchange rates**

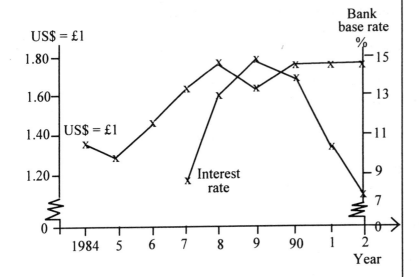

19.2   **Describe the main instruments that are available to help manage the volatility of such rates**

❏   Interest rates

  ❏   interest rate futures
  ❏   forward rate agreements (FRAs)
  ❏   interest rate options
  ❏   interest rate swaps
  ❏   swaptions

❏   Exchange rates

  ❏   forward foreign exchange contracts (dealt with above)

  ❏   futures contracts

  ❏   option contracts

  ❏   currency swaps

19.3   **Explain the nature of futures contracts**

❏   Definition

  A futures contract is an agreement to buy or sell a standard quantity of a particular financial instrument on a predetermined future date at a price agreed now.

❏   futures contracts are traded on exchanges such as LIFFE

19.4 Discuss the use of margin requirements and the functions of futures clearing houses

❑ initial margin - payable on starting the contract

❑ vai iatlon margin - paid/received each day as the contract is marked to market

❑ clearing houses - each futures exchange uses a clearing house to guarantee each party's performance of their side of each contract.

19.5 Explain how price movements are recognised within futures markets

❑ a tick is the minimum price movement permitted for each contract

❑ price movements are then stated in numbers of ticks

Example

The LIFFE short-term 3 month sterling interest rate futures contract has a contract value of £500,000 and a tick size of 0.01% (so that prices are quoted in numbers and hundredths of a per cent).

The tick value is therefore $0.01\% \times \frac{3}{12} \times £500,000 = £12.50$. If you own 10 contracts and the price of a contract rises from 94.20 to 95.30, each contract has risen in price by 110 ticks (being 110 hundredths of a per cent) and your total profit is

10 contracts × 110 ticks × £12.50/tick
=   £13,750

19.6 Describe the major interest rate futures (short-term and long-term) and currency futures contracts

❑ Interest rate futures on LIFFE

	Contract value	Tick size
3 month sterling	£500,000	0.01%
3 month eurodollar	$1m	0.01%
3 month euromark	DM 1m	0.01%
9% notional UK gilt	£50,000	$\frac{1}{32}$ of £1
8% US Treasury Bond	$100,000	$\frac{1}{32}$ of $1
6% notional German Bond	DM 250,000	$\frac{1}{100}$ of DM1

❑ Currency futures on IMM

$/£	£62,500	0.01c/£
$/Swiss franc	SF 125,000	0.01c/SF

19.7   Evaluate hedging strategies with both interest rate and currency futures using given information

❑   hedging with a futures contract means that the profit/loss on an underlying instrument (eg, on a holding of foreign currency) will be equal and opposite to the loss/profit on the futures contract, so that risk has been eliminated.

❑   a perfect hedge exactly covers the risk; this is unlikely since contracts are only available in large round-sum quantities of each instrument. It is usual to over-hedge and round up the required number of contracts to the whole number above.

19.8   Contrast the use of currency futures with forward contracts

Futures	*Forwards*
Traded on an exchange	Arranged through a bank
Standard sizes and dates only	Organised specifically as required
Initial margin required	No margin requirement
Hedging may be incomplete	Eliminates currency risk

Session 20   Options

20.1   Describe the main features of options including puts and calls, the exercise price, American and European options, in and out of the money

Definition

An option contract provides the purchaser with the right but not the obligation to buy from/sell to the seller of the option a fixed amount of a financial instrument in the future at a price fixed today

❑   the seller of the option is called the writer

❑   the price fixed in the contract at which the instrument can be bought/sold is called the exercise price

❑   an option to buy is a call option

❑   an option to sell is a put option

❑   the purchaser pays a premium to buy the option

❑   European options may be exercised only on a specific date

❑   American options may be exercised on any day between two dates (the option period)

❑   a call option is in the money if the current market price is above the exercise price.

❑   a call option is out of the money if the current market price is below the exercise price

❑   a put option is in the money if the current market price is below the exercise price

❑   a put option is out of the money if the current market price is above the exercise price

❑   options are at the money if the current market price equals the exercise price

20.2   Differentiate between traded options and over-the-counter options

Options can either be exchange traded in standard sizes eg, on LIFFE, or individually designed as OTC contracts.

Exchange traded options have a readily quoted market price but are only available in standard sizes in a limited number of exercise prices, a limited number of expiry dates and a limited number of underlying instruments.

OTC options are infinitely variable, capable of being designed to specific requirements.

20.3   Discuss the determinants of option prices, including the Black-Scholes model and its limitations

❑   value of an option =

intrinsic value   +   time value

↑   ↑

positive if in the   increases as
money   the time to
                             maturity
                             increases

Determinants of the price of an option

❑   whether a call or put

❑   whether European or American

❑   the current market price of the underlying instrument

❑   the exercise price

❑   the risk free rate of interest

❑   the time to expiry

❑   the volatility of the price of the instrument, measured by the standard deviation of the instrument's returns.

Don't panic when faced with the Black-Scholes equation. You will not have to use the equation in the exam, but only to be aware that it uses the determinants listed above in its construction. A basic (!) form for the value of a European call option is:

$$\text{Option price} = PN(d_1) - Xe^{-rt} N(d_2)$$

$$\text{where} \quad d_1 = \frac{\log_e\left(\frac{P}{X}\right) + \left(r + \frac{\sigma^2}{2}\right)t}{\sigma\sqrt{t}}$$

$$d_2 = d_1 - \sigma\sqrt{t}$$

Symbols used

P   =   price of the underlying instrument

$N(d_i)$ =   probability that a normal distribution is less than d_i

X   =   exercise price

r   =   risk free interest rate

t   =   time to expiry

σ =   standard deviation of the instrument's returns

Limitations of the basic Black-Scholes model

❑   assumes no dividends are paid in the period of option

❑   only applies to European options

❑   risk free rate is constant throughout the option's life

❑ σ is constant through time

❑   there are no transaction costs or tax effects

Certain of these limitations can be removed by more sophisticated versions of the model.

20.4   Explain the advantages and disadvantages of options compared to futures

Options	*v*	*Futures and forwards*
Offer participation in favourable movements, but premiums must be paid		Guarantee future costs or revenues
Useful when underlying trade position is uncertain (ie, if deal falls through option could be abandoned)		Must be delivered

20.5 **Describe the various types of interest rate options, including short-term options, caps, collars and floors, and the nature of currency options**

Interest rate options

❑ LIFFE interest rate option contracts involve an option over interest rate futures contracts and are priced in ticks as already described. For example the short sterling option gives options over £500,000 in points of 100% (ie, the tick size is 0.01%).

❑ OTC interest rate option contracts can be short-term (called an interest rate guarantee) or long-term (caps, collars and floors)

Caps - protection against interest rate rises above a cap rate

Floors - protection against interest rate falls below a floor rate

Collars - a simultaneous cap and floor position

Currency options

❑ the right, but not the obligation, to buy or sell a particular currency at a specified exchange rate in the future

20.6 **Be aware of the nature and benefits of low cost or zero cost options**

❑ it is possible to reduce the premium payable on options by reducing the possible benefits that may be received

❑ a cylinder option involves buying and writing options on the same quantity of instrument at different exercise prices. The put premium received offsets the call premium paid.

20.7   Evaluate alternative hedging scenarios using interest rate and currency options

	Problem	*Futures*	*Options*
(i)	UK company has a $ debtor	Buy £ futures and company will lock into a fixed exchange rate	Buy call options and company will have the option to buy £ at exercise price. If cheaper on the spot market, options can be abandoned
(ii)	UK company thinks £ will strengthen and wishes to speculate	Buy £ futures (buy £ forward) and profit as £ rises above the fixed rate	Buy call options and profit as £ rises above the exercise price, if not abandon. Alternatively, sell (write) put options and pocket the premium as no one exercises
(iii)	UK company needs to borrow £'s in future	Sell £ interest rate futures (sell forward) giving obligation to sell bonds (borrow money) at fixed interest	Buy put options on £ interest rate futures giving option to sell bonds (borrow money) at exercise price. If interest rates fall, abandon
(iv)	UK company wishes to invest £'s in a diversified portfolio of equities in the future	Buy FTSE100 futures and lock into a fixed price portfolio	Buy call options on FTSE100 futures giving option to buy portfolio at exercise price. If market falls abandon

Session 21   *Swaps*

21.1   Describe nature of interest rate and currency swaps

The parties to a swap contract agree to exchange cashflows over an agreed period of time.

- interest rate swap

    - from fixed to floating rates, and vice versa

- currency swap

    - exchange of the interest payments payable on liabilities denominated in different currencies

21.2   Understand the value of swaps to the corporate treasurer

- access to capital markets unaccessible directly

- cheaper interest rates

- change the structure of a company's debt liabilities. In 1993 the reducing levels of interest rates have led to many companies swapping fixed to floating rate debt.

- hedging currency risks

21.3   Understand the role of banks in swap activity

- the two parties use a bank as an intermediary

- the bank can either contract with each party, or stand back and just take an arrangement fee

21.4   Describe the various types of risk that are associated with swaps

- credit risk
- market risk
- sovereign risk

Banks arranging swaps are exposed to

- mismatch risk
- basis risk

21.5 Describe hybrid forms of instruments such as swaptions, and the value of financial engineering

Definitions

Swaptions are option contracts on swaps. They give the right, but not the obligation, to enter into an interest rate swap on or before a fixed date.

- ❑ payer swaptions

- ❑ receiver swaptions

- ❑ can be European or American

- ❑ OTC, so are specifically tailored to each party's requirements

Financial engineering is the process of combining together different financial instruments to produce a new financial instrument.

- ❑ Examples

  - ❑ zero cost options can be created by combining the buying with the writing of options at different exercise prices

  - ❑ synthetic stocks can be created by combining options which can then be arbitraged against. Eg, buy a call and sell a put to create a synthetic long and then take arbitrage profits by selling the stock and holding the synthetic long.

21.6 Evaluate hedging scenarios using swaps and swaptions

Possible swap strategies include the following:

Interest rate swaps (normally in one currency)

Conversions: H Borough Council has borrowed fixed rate and it suspects interest rates will fall. Swaps with a bank whereby bank takes on fixed interest payments and council pays bank variable interest rate (LIBOR + x%). Winner is determined by future interest rate changes.

Comparative advantage: A plc can borrow more cheaply than B plc at both fixed and variable rates, however its biggest advantage is on fixed rate. Applying comparative advantage A should borrow fixed, B variable and swap - both parties will win.

Currency swaps

Assume a UK company wished to obtain a FF loan and a French company wished to obtain a £ loan and their credit status was better at home than abroad. If they both borrowed on their domestic home currency and then swapped (ie, UK company pays FF interest and French company pays £ interest) they would both gain from each other's credit standing. Principal could be repaid at spot rates or via a forward contract to give foreign exchange protection

Session 22   Transfer pricing

22.1   Explain the importance of transfer pricing to multinational companies

    (a)   Needs, aims and problems

❑   Needs

Needed if a firm has decentralised and goods or services are transferred between divisions

❑   Aims

    ❑   To divide total corporate profit between divisional profit centres

    ❑   To provide input data for decision-making

    ❑   To help assess the performance of divisional managers

❑   Problems

    ❑   Inter-divisional disputes over suitability of price

    ❑   Lack of motivation if price produces divisional losses

    ❑   Dysfunctional decisions made by local managers (lack of goal congruence)

    (b)   Practical methods of transfer pricing

❑   Market based prices
❑   Cost-related prices
❑   Negotiated prices
❑   Dual prices

22.2   Understand the legal regulations affecting transfer pricing, particularly with respect to the attitude of tax authorities

❑   overall objective may be to maximise total international tax bill

❑   want to report low profits in high tax areas and vice versa

❑   recognising this, most countries require transfer prices to be set on an arm's length basis

❑   note that the aim of minimising tax may run contrary to the other aims identified above including motivation.

22.3 **Discuss the use of tax havens to try to maximise the benefits of transfer pricing**

Definitions

A tax haven is a country which imposes low rates of tax

This implies

- ❑ low corporation tax rates
- ❑ low withholding taxes on dividends paid
- ❑ favourable tax treaties with other countries

22.4 **Explain the potential adverse motivational effects of transfer pricing on individual subsidiaries or divisions**

- ❑ the aim of minimising total tax may mean that head office must impose a transfer price between two divisions, resulting in

  - ❑ one division reporting lower profits than if they had bought the transferred items on the open market. This will displease divisional management

  - ❑ imposing prices from on high reduces divisional autonomy

- ❑ problems will be avoided if transfer prices are set at the external market price.

22.5 **Describe the guidelines appropriate to the regular financial reports required from overseas operations**

- ❑ prepared on a consistent basis

- ❑ financial and non-financial information should be included

- ❑ translate according to SSAP 20

- ❑ proper flexible budgeting system

22.6 **Evaluate the performance of all or part of an international group of companies using ratio and other forms of analysis**

Key performance measures

- ❑ absolute actual level of profits (and compared with budget)

- ❑ absolute actual level of sales (and compared with budget)

❑   return on investment

❑   residual income

Note the comparison between the final two.

(i)   Return on Investment

$$\text{ROI} = \frac{\text{Controllable Profit}}{\text{Controllable Investment}} \times 100$$

Limitations

❑   Subject to accounting policies

❑   Identification of controllable profit

      ❑   Treatment of depreciation

      ❑   Exclusion of apportionment of central costs

      ❑   Controllable quantities but price set centrally

      ❑   Assessing controllability of tax

❑   Determination of controllable investment

      ❑   Normally includes working capital

      ❑   Some fixed assets may be excluded if managed centrally

❑   Valuation of controllable investment

      ❑   Original cost: may lead to a tendency to dispose of an asset prematurely

      ❑   Net book value: may lead to a reluctance to dispose of an asset

      ❑   Current value: preferable

❑   May lead to decision making which conflicts with DCF methods

(ii)   Residual income

❑   RI   =   Controllable profit less an imputed interest

Advantages

❑   Generally consistent with DCF techniques if the cost of capital is used to compute the interest charge

❑ Divisional managers made aware of the costs of finance

Limitations

❑ Determining suitable cost of capital to cover fixed asset and working capital investment

❑ WACC may not be suitable as it does not reflect the risk of individual division

❑ Determination of controllable profit and investment as for ROI

Session 23   *The International Treasury Function*

23.1   Discuss the merits of defining the treasury as a cost centre or profit centre

The international treasury function obtains finance on a world-wide basis and controls the uses of that finance.

As a cost centre the aggregate treasury function costs would simply be charged throughout the group on a fair basis. If no such fair basis can be agreed, the costs can remain as central unallocated costs in any segmental analysis.

However the trend in recent years has been for multinational companies to establish their treasury functions as profit centres.

This may involve:

❑   charging divisions the opportunity cost of the treasury services, which should exceed their costs, in order to report a profit

❑   not hedging all risks. Experts in the treasury could decide which risks not to hedge, hoping to profit from favourable exchange rate and interest rate movements

❑   hedging using currency options to leave an upside potential

❑   taking on additional exchange rate risks purely as a speculative activity

❑   such activities must be properly controlled; see the case of Allied-Lyons losing £150m if you are not convinced.

Conclusion

As long as speculative activities are controlled by management, creating the treasury function as a profit centre can bring substantial rewards.

23.2   Discuss the arguments for centralisation versus the decentralisation of international treasury activities

Factors to consider

❑   adverse motivational effects of centralisation

❑   better returns available on cash held centrally

❑   practicality of hedging strategies

❑   skills of specialised treasury experts (members of ACT)

    ❑   setting of transfer prices

    ❑   local knowledge of local opportunities

23.3 Describe the main forms of international cash transfer mechanisms

    ❑   SWIFT
    ❑   CHIPS
    ❑   EFT
    ❑   EDI
    ❑   Letter of credit
    ❑   Bill of exchange

23.4 Describe the short term investment opportunities that exist in international money markets and in international marketable securities

    ❑   short term bank deposits
    ❑   Eurocurrency deposits
    ❑   CDs
    ❑   Treasury Bills
    ❑   trade bills and bank bills
    ❑   commercial paper
    ❑   UK local authority bills and deposits
    ❑   federal funds (advances to US banks)

Session 24 *International Operations*

24.1 **Describe the forms of entity that are available for international operations, including the relative merits of branch, subsidiary, joint venture, licensing and economic interest groups**

❑ export from the home country

  ❑ advantages: cheap, low risk

  ❑ disadvantages: hard to get a feel for the market, high cost of travel for salesforce

❑ set up an overseas branch

  ❑ advantages: cheap, quick method to set up a local presence

  ❑ disadvantages: tax

❑ set up an overseas subsidiary

  ❑ advantages: can establish transfer prices, profits taxed abroad

  ❑ disadvantages: cost of a long-term commitment

❑ joint venture

  ❑ advantages: pool expertise, reduce risk

  ❑ disadvantages: run for whose interests? technology transfer, time involved

❑ licensing

  ❑ advantages: cheap, quick, reduces political risk

  ❑ disadvantages: fixed period of time, technology transfer

❑ Economic Interest Groups (EIGs)

  ❑ eg, European Economic Interest Groupings

  ❑ facilitate co-operation between firms based in different countries

  ❑ advantages: governed by a common law rather than the law of individual countries, legal entity in their own right

  ❑ disadvantages: time involved

24.2   Discuss the complexities of foreign direct investment, including the possible forms and implications of political risk and its importance to the investment decision process

❑   Political risk

   ❑   Varies from expropriation of assets to blockages on remission of funds to requirements for local ownership or employment

   ❑   Protection -   Avoid establishing a complete unit overseas (eg, keep R&D, component manufacture, distribution channels under parent control)

                  -    Borrow locally

                  -    Prior negotiations

                  -    Be a good citizen of host country

❑   Discount rate

   ❑   Diversification possibilities might decrease risk rather than increasing it, discount rates are difficult to determine

❑   Financing

   ❑   Packages should protect against political and forex risk

   ❑   Parent equity gives little protection, local loans give protection against both risks

24.3   Discuss the impact of blocked funds and restrictions on the remittance of funds to the parent company, and the use of royalties, management charges etc, to avoid restrictions on remittances.

❑   Blocked funds

   These are funds that the company is prevented from remitting back to the holding company country.

   ❑   exchange controls might prevent conversion of a currency

   ❑   an overseas government might freeze particular bank accounts

❑   Remission of funds

       ❑   Dividends (most politically sensitive)
       ❑   Royalties
       ❑   Transfer prices, supervisory fees
       ❑   Inter company loans

Session 25   *International Capital Budgeting*

25.1   Estimate the international cost of capital for an organisation, using the CAPM

- ❏   CAPM identifies systematic risk and unsystematic risk, suggests that unsystematic risk can be diversified away, and defines β as a measure of an investment's systematic risk

- ❏   a firm involved internationally may be exposed to

    - ❏   currency risk
    - ❏   political risk

    These are unsystematic and can be diversified away

- ❏   international diversification can further reduce systematic risk since a portfolio of international shares will have lower systematic risk than a portfolio of just UK shares

- ❏   international diversification can be achieved by

    - ❏   direct holdings in overseas companies

    - ❏   holdings in unit trusts specialising in overseas companies

    - ❏   investing in multinational companies

- ❏   when using CAPM to estimate the required return that a company should seek from a new project, beta should be calculated for the industry and the country in which the project will be engaged

25.2   Evaluate how APV might be used in international investment appraisal

APV method

Step 1   Calculate the base case NPV

Step 2   Calculate the present value of financing side effects

Step 3   APV = sum of steps 1 and 2. If positive, accept.

- ❏   there are additional possible side effects when the APV method is used in international investment appraisal:

    - ❏   subsidies from foreign governments
    - ❏   project financed by loans raised locally
    - ❏   restrictions on remittance

25.3 Illustrate the effect of taxation on international investment, including the possibility of double taxation

❑ Effects of taxation will be described in the question and may include:

    ❑ capital allowances
    ❑ different tax rates in UK and overseas country
    ❑ double tax agreements
    ❑ corporation tax payable one year in arrears

❑ Normally a double tax agreement permits a UK company to claim a credit for overseas tax suffered, up to a maximum of the UK rate.

25.4 Discuss the advantages and disadvantages of international portfolio diversification

❑ advantages

    ❑ reduces systematic risk

    ❑ international CAPM suggests greater returns are possible from any agreed risk level

❑ disadvantages

    ❑ may increase total risk

    ❑ problem of whether investor should invest directly in overseas companies or in a multinational

    ❑ tax complications

Session 26   The International Capital Structure Decision

26.1   Discuss the factors that influence the type of finance used in international operations

Separate problems deal with

❑   the financing of the holding company

    ❑   foreign loans to hedge overseas net investment

❑   the financing of overseas branches/subsidiaries

    ❑   size of equity investment

    ❑   large equity investment implies long-term commitment

    ❑   minority shareholding, or small equity combined with large debt raised locally, suggests short-term horizon

    ❑   management of working capital

The holding company will probably wish to hedge its currency risk exposure. It can either do this by raising foreign loans in its own books, or by requiring subsidiaries to match their exposures as much as possible.

26.2   Describe the strategic implications of international financing, with respect both to the type of finance used, and the currency in which the financing is denominated

❑   as mentioned above, the more the equity content of the financing package, the longer the perceived investment horizon

❑   multinational companies will wish to carry out foreign direct investments for the following strategic reasons:

    ❑   gain access to foreign markets
    ❑   direct access to raw materials
    ❑   seeking cheap factors of production
    ❑   retention of technological expertise

❑   the financing will be denominated in the currency required to satisfy the overall hedging strategy, as discussed above.

26.3   **Undertake a detailed appraisal of an international capital investment proposal using given information - this could be either by organic growth or acquisition**

Normal NPV rules apply. The assumed objective of shareholder wealth maximisation requires the relevant cash flows to be discounted at the appropriate discount rate.

Problems are likely to arise in dealing with overseas inflation rates and tax regimes. The question 'Axmine plc' in the Paper 14 pilot paper covers this topic well.

ACCA

AT FOULKS LYNCH

HOTLINES
Telephone: 0181 844 0667
Fax: 0181 831 9991

AT FOULKS LYNCH LTD
Number 4, The Griffin Centre
Staines Road, Feltham
Middlesex TW14 0HS

Examination Date: Dec 96 ☐ Jun 97 ☐	Textbooks	Revision Series	Exam Notes	Distance Learning (Includes all materials)	Open Learning	Helpline & Marking (For Open Learning)
Module A - Foundation Stage						
1 Accounting Framework	£17 ☐	£9 ☐	£5 ☐	£85 ☐	£99 ☐	£20 ☐
2 Legal Framework	£17 ☐	£9 ☐	£5 ☐	£85 ☐	£99 ☐	£20 ☐
Module B						
3 Management Information	£17 ☐	£9 ☐	£5 ☐	£85 ☐	£99 ☐	£20 ☐
4 Organisational Framework	£17 ☐	£9 ☐	£5 ☐	£85 ☐	£99 ☐	£20 ☐
Module C - Certificate Stage						
5 Information Analysis	£17 ☐	£9 ☐	£5 ☐	£85 ☐	£99 ☐	£20 ☐
6 Audit Framework	£17 ☐	£9 ☐	£5 ☐	£85 ☐	£99 ☐	£20 ☐
Module D						
7 Tax Framework (FA96)	£17 ☐	£9 ☐	£5 ☐	£85 ☐	£99 ☐	£20 ☐
8 Managerial Finance	£17 ☐	£9 ☐	£5 ☐	£85 ☐	£99 ☐	£20 ☐
Module E - Professional Stage						
9 ICDM	£18 ☐	£9 ☐	£5 ☐	£85 ☐	£99 ☐	£20 ☐
10 Accounting & Audit Practice	£20 ☐	£9 ☐	£5 ☐	£85 ☐	£99 ☐	£20 ☐
11 Tax Planning (FA96)	£18 ☐	£9 ☐	£5 ☐	£85 ☐	£99 ☐	£20 ☐
Module F						
12 Management & Strategy	£18 ☐	£9 ☐	£5 ☐	£85 ☐	£99 ☐	£20 ☐
13 Financial Rep Environment	£18 ☐	£9 ☐	£5 ☐	£85 ☐	£99 ☐	£20 ☐
14 Financial Strategy	£18 ☐	£9 ☐	£5 ☐	£85 ☐	£99 ☐	£20 ☐
TOTAL Sub Total £						
Postage £						
Total £						

POSTAGE						
UK Mainland	£2.00/book	£1.00/book	£1.00/book	£5.00/pack	£5.00/pack	
NI, ROI & Europe	£5.00/book	£3.00/book	£3.00/book	£15.00/pack	£15.00/pack	
Rest of World Standard Service	£10.00/book	£8.00/book	£8.00/book	£25.00/pack	£25.00/pack	Postage Free
COURIER China & Asia	£20.00/book	£17.00/book	£12.00/book	£44.00/pack	£44.00/pack	
West Indies & Africa	£23.00/book	£20.00/book	£14.00/book	£47.00/pack	£47.00/pack	
Far East & Middle East	£17.00/book	£15.00/book	£11.00/book	£34.00/pack	£34.00/pack	
SINGLE ITEM POSTAGE	For orders of 1 item only, add £2.50 (UK & Europe) or £10.00 (Rest of World)					

DELIVERY DETAILS

Student's name (print)

Delivery address

Postcode

Country   Tel (Home)

Tel (Day)   Fax

Note: All delivery times subject to stock availability.
Signature required on receipt.
Allow: 5 working days - work address (UK mainland)
10 working days - home address (UK mainland)
6 weeks for Overseas Standard Service

DECLARATION

I agree to pay as indicated on this form and understand that AT Foulks Lynch Ltd Terms and Conditions apply (available on request). I understand that AT Foulks Lynch Ltd are not liable for non-delivery if the Rest of World Standard Air Service is used.

Signature   Date

PAYMENT OPTIONS

1. I enclose Cheque/PO/Bankers Draft for £_____

Please make cheques payable to AT Foulks Lynch Ltd.

2. Charge Access/Visa Account Number

☐☐☐☐☐☐☐☐☐☐☐☐☐☐☐☐

Expiry Date ☐☐☐☐

Signature   Date

3. Please invoice employer. Minimum order of £150.
30 days credit. I agree to pay fees of £_____

Name (print)

Position

Signature

Company Name

Invoice Address

Post Code   Country

Telephone   Fax

All details correct at time of printing.

Source: ACNTJ6